*This book is dedicated to my Mom and Dad
and to all the older people who carry a lifetime
of wisdom within them.*

Contents

Introduction   1

CHAPTER ONE
Investment Advice: The Guardian Angel
Syndrome   5

CHAPTER TWO
Avoiding Estates of Confusions: Trusts vs. Wills 22

CHAPTER THREE
Joint Tenancy with Right of Survivorship
and Gifting   49

CHAPTER FOUR
Durable Power of Attorney for Health Care   68

CHAPTER FIVE
Long-Term-Care Insurance: Pay Now or
Pay (a Lot More) Later   79

CHAPTER SIX
Early Retirement   104

CHAPTER SEVEN
Joint and Survivor Benefits   135

CHAPTER EIGHT
Minimize Your Expenses/Maximize Your Income 163

CHAPTER NINE
A Successful Retirement   194

Glossary   195

Resources   206

Index   220

Acknowledgments

It takes a lifetime of people to create a book. The spirit of all those retired individuals whom I have met or who became my clients has always made it such a joy to want to do the best for them. I cherish the wonderful people who allowed us to interview them for this book.

For their expertise and whose professionalism I highly regard, I'd like to thank Janet Dobrovolny, Professor Phil Storrer, Dr. Jerry Kasner, Timothy Millar, Gail Mitchell, Eleanor Calamari, and Sharon Janis.

For reading the manuscript in its various stages and their refreshing comments, I'm grateful to Melissa Howden, Caryn Dickman, Kai Ekhammer, Paula Canny, A. Nevin Mercede, Kumuda, Doris Wolff, Noni Colhoun, Woody Simmons, Laurie Brown Nayder, Cynthia Oti, and Howard Fisher. And to all my other friends for their unyielding support.

For those who felt this book worthy of their endorsement, our heartfelt thanks.

For her hospitality and use of her cottage where this book came together, thanks to Damaris Ethridge of Landmark Vineyards.

For having faith in this project and continuous encouragement, our publisher Esther Margolis and editor Keith Hollaman.

For helping make this dream a reality, I am particularly appreciative of the tireless efforts of my agent, coauthor, and friend Linda Mead.

For putting up with the long hours on the phone and separations, a hug to my partner and to Linda's husband.

For my dear friend Ruth Carnovsky, whose age has only increased her spark of brilliance.

And most especially to Gurumayi, who has taught me that doing what is right is far better than doing what is easy.

This publication is designed to provide accurate and authoritative information in regard to the subject matter covered. It is published with the understanding that the publisher and author are not engaged in rendering legal accounting or other professional service. If legal advice or other professional advice, including financial, is required, the services of a competent professional person should be sought.

> —From a Declaration of Principles, jointly adopted by a Committee of the American Bar Association and a Committee of Publishers

Introduction

WHAT DOES IT TAKE to get people to understand they could suffer financial ruin if they don't take a few simple measures to protect their retirement? The answer: financial ruin. In my practice, when I tell people that there are steps they must take to protect themselves, they can't imagine that anything could happen to them. They can't identify with the issues of potential misfortune, so they just don't deal with it.

Each day, though, we open the newspaper or turn on the TV and learn about someone else's retirement woes. There had to be something I could do to address this widespread situation. Thus this book, laced with real-life stories meant to engage you, even shock you into action in a format that answers your questions, explores possibilities, creates a deeper understanding, and gives you hope. More than anything else, though, this book's purpose is to help you protect your future—everything you have worked for, saved for, and plan to enjoy.

For those of you who don't think you have to be concerned about this, let me be the first to caution you. I can't tell you how often I encounter people who pour their hearts out about themselves or someone else who has lost their retirement money for one reason or another. In the pages of this book you will find their stories, filled with all the fears, anxieties, and pain that financial inadequacy can cause. These people have agreed to share their experiences with us, to wave a red flag of warning in front of our faces, to wake us up before it's too late. I thank them for that. I only wish I could have reached these people before things went wrong.

Retirement is one of the most critical domestic issues facing our country today. The topic covers a broad range of financial, emotional, and health care concerns that must be addressed. Until we can depend on a system that protects and cares for its elderly, it will be up to each and every one of us to take care of our own financial futures.

This book deals with some very basic issues that will directly affect the financial and emotional outcome of your retirement. Some of these issues include:

• *Financial advisors:* The last thing anyone should do is hand over a fistful of cash to a broker who promises to be a guardian angel, but it happens.

• *Trusts, wills, and joint tenancy:* It is a shame to see people lose their home or other acquired assets. Your home and your belongings need to be protected for your sake as well as for your children who will receive them when you are gone. It does your children no good to inherit property they may have to sell to pay probate fees or taxes.

• *Early retirement and joint and survivor benefits:* Retirement doesn't necessarily mean sixty-five anymore. The floodgates have been opened with layoffs and forced early retirement, so any age is retirement age, as you will see with my client Doug, who was stunned by the prospect of early retirement and paralyzed from the fear of making the wrong decisions.

• *Long-term care:* What about the possibility of a long-term-care stay for your parent or perhaps yourself sometime in the future? Are you prepared for that? Most people aren't. In fact, the majority of people believe that Medicare or their health insurance will pay for all or part of a long-term-care stay. They will not. As our aging population increases, the need for nursing-home care will soar proportionately, as will the cost of a long-term-care stay. And beds will be at a premium. Can you honestly say you can afford $2,000, $3,000, or $4,000 a month for this kind of care for your elderly parent or yourself?

Your money and the safety of your retirement require that you take control of your destiny. This book will help you do just that.

Although we address most of the issues in this book to those who are retired or about to retire, let me stress that this is not a retirement book, nor is it a financial book. *It is a lifestyle book that deals with the financial issues of retirement,* because those issues affect every member of a retiree's family, be it wife or husband, partner, children or aging parents. As you will see from the very beginning of the book, the children of retirees are especially affected by their parents' decisions and are just as vulnerable to loss due to these decisions. So this book is important for the children of the retired, too. Share this book with your children, since they will be an integral part of your choices.

Share this book with your professional advisors— your lawyer, tax consultant, financial planner, and the director of your local office on aging—since these people will be crucial in aiding you.

Retirement is a special time. Like adolescence or adulthood or parenthood, it marks another turning point on the path of life. It is a new beginning, a rejuvenation, not the retreat from life or work, as conventional wisdom would have us believe, now that the average life span extends twenty or thirty years beyond retirement. It is a time to look forward.

To help you stay on your path, we have prepared

the chapters of this book in an easy-to-use format so you may reference specific information anytime you wish. Each personal story is followed by a discussion of the case, which, in turn, is followed by detailed guidelines. Each chapter is designed to give you the information and the tools you will need to protect yourself, your retirement, and your future.

SUZE ORMAN

Investment Advice: The Guardian Angel Syndrome

I have no money left! How can that be? I gave them my money to invest, not lose!

Anita's Story

When my husband died in 1974 I received $10,000 from his GI insurance policy. I know it wasn't much, but I took this money and some money I borrowed from my younger sister and made a down payment on a small house in Kensington, California, for my son John and me.

Four years later, when I turned sixty, I finally retired from my job as a library assistant. Shortly afterward, I received a small inheritance from my older sister's estate. When the money arrived, I decided to invest it because the temptation to spend it would have been too great. I decided to go to a large, well-known brokerage firm with a local office in Berkeley. I thought of them because I saw their ad in the newspaper. It pictured a young, blond woman standing in an office doorway. The caption under her picture read GUARDIAN ANGEL in big letters. And under that it quoted, "I have a lot of retired folks for clients who give me more than just money to invest. They give me their trust." So when I arrived at that company, I asked for a woman broker just like the one in the ad. That's when I met Patti.

Patti was totally convincing. She had such a winning way about her. She was so gracious and welcoming. Never the least bit insulting. She insisted she would tell me everything I needed to know and would take care of everything. She was reassuring on every level.

Patti explained that she and her partner monitored the stocks of some fifty companies and knew exactly where and when to invest and when to pull out. They were on top of things all the time. Additionally, she said that she got a yearly return of 40 percent to 45 percent on her personal investments and, even though I couldn't expect as high a return, I could get about 20 percent to 25 percent. Well, CDs were up to 14 percent at the time. So I thought that maybe I could make this much.

The only stipulation I had for Patti was that she keep my money safe and sound, so I wouldn't lose it. We agreed, and she then gave me blank account forms for my son and me to sign as joint tenants in case of my death. The account was officially opened, and because I trusted Patti, I left everything in her hands and didn't pay much attention to it after that. I felt like I had a daughter looking after me.

In 1981 my son John considered a career move to Los Angeles. After some discussion, we decided to sell the house because I just didn't want to live there by myself. It was a little too remote in the Berkeley hills, and since I didn't drive . . . besides, the house had tripled in value. We finally sold it in October 1982 and received $160,000. This was more money than I had ever seen in my life. Once Patti invested it for me, it would give me substantially more income to live on. And, being a retired library assistant, I could really use the additional income. All I had was Social Security, a small pension, and my investment with Patti.

As a temporary measure after the house was sold, I set myself up in a small rental apartment in Santa Cruz. It took some time to get used to such a small place, but I really thought it would only be temporary. It never occurred to me that all the mail I was receiving from Patti's office meant there might be

something wrong. I assumed it meant she was working on my behalf.

Discussion

A<small>NITA CAME TO ME</small> through the encouragement of one of her friends, who thought
something was indeed wrong. Anita confessed that she
was having trouble understanding her statements, but
Patti would send handwritten notes adding up everything for her. It wasn't until Anita's friend, Ellen, no-
ticed that the figures on the notes didn't coincide with
the numbers on the statements that Anita was encour-
aged to call Patti for an explanation. She was told not
to worry, that there was so much activity that the statements were never up to the minute. Even when Anita
asked for a list of her investments, Patti's excuses for
not sending it were believable. This went on for
months. Even though Anita was somewhat annoyed,
she never suspected anything was really wrong. She
said she always trusted Patti to take care of her.

To find out what really happened here, I needed
more information. I asked Anita to gather everything
relating to her account. She returned after a few days
with a box of paperwork in hand.

When I looked at her statements I was shocked to
discover that Anita had no money left. How was I going
to tell her that? We continued sifting through the papers, sorting and dissecting every piece to complete the
puzzle. I determined that hundreds of trades had been
made in Anita's account. Her broker had been buying
options—one of the most speculative investments anyone can make. Since 90 percent of all people who buy
options lose their money, how was it possible that this
brokerage firm had allowed Anita to invest in options?
All firms have strict financial requirements that clients

must meet before entering into risky investments. I knew Anita didn't qualify, so I had her request all the original paperwork she had signed to open up the account. All the figures that gave Anita's net worth were dramatically inflated so she could qualify to buy options. Patti overstated Anita's net worth by $250,000. Since the forms were signed by Anita before the inclusion of these figures, the brokerage firm and Anita had no way of knowing the figures had been fabricated. I began to wonder what else had been falsified.

The main mistake Anita made was that *she signed blank papers she did not read or understand.* Anita had signed on and checked out, leaving the broker in charge of all her money.

In a case such as this, Anita's only avenue to recoup some of her losses was arbitration. (For information on arbitration, see the Resources section in the back of this book.) From all the money given to Patti to invest, more than three hundred trades were made on Anita's account from 1981 to 1984, an exorbitant number by any standards. Patti had made thousands and thousands of dollars in commissions, and Anita was left with nothing. Even though the arbitration committee ruled in favor of Anita, after paying one third in attorney's fees, as well as other debts she incurred over the time it took to come to settlement, Anita was left with $50,000, a far cry from her original amount. Today an arbitration board can award far more than they gave Anita, because they now tend to award punitive damages.

If Anita's investments had been prudently made— even if she had simply left her money in a money market fund—because interest rates were so high then, she would have been $100,000 ahead. Instead of having $50,000 to her name, Anita would have $270,000, generating more than enough interest in income for her to live comfortably. Her old age would have been safe and secure.

What went wrong in Anita's case started long before her husband died. Anita, like many wives of her generation, depended on her husband's knowledge of finances. Even though she had the wherewithal to invest the inheritance from her sister and the profit from the sale of her house, she needed to learn about money, and she needed to be accountable personally for the management of her funds.

Anita's desire *to be taken care of* lured her into the arms of an unscrupulous broker. To be taken in by an advertising campaign, a warm smile, a reassuring manner, and the hopes of a guardian angel was a deadly mistake. Seek out advisors who come personally recommended by others who use them. When you choose your place of worship, you go to a place that befits your beliefs. You find your doctor through others who have been there. You have even decided on a favorite supermarket because it has the best quality and prices. How do you know these things? Comparison shopping. You've checked them out, or they have been recommended by others. So why would you select someone you know nothing about to invest your money?

Anita's problems were compounded because she feared being judged or made to feel inadequate. She wouldn't dare question a professional, so she never learned how to read the statements or apprise herself of what was happening with her account, even when she received conflicting notices.

Today, at seventy-four, Anita lives on an income of $1,100 per month, with fixed expenses of $900 per month. How is her life different? Anita explains, "To go to the airport, I take four buses and a train. It only costs three to four dollars with my senior discounts, but it takes five hours. A cab costs forty dollars. I do all my shopping in thrift shops. I never go to a department store to buy anything new— ever."

Guidelines

Here are some simple guidelines to help you avoid the guardian angel syndrome.

There are several steps you will want to take when seeking the best financial advisor. They include preparing for the interview, interviewing and selecting an advisor, opening an account, and monitoring it. If you take the time to prepare in advance, it will be well worth the effort.

PREPARING FOR THE INTERVIEW

Both you and your spouse or significant other should address the following issues:

1. Clarify your goals before you see an advisor. Do you want to travel? Take vacations? Sell your house and buy a mobile home? Buy a new car? Redo your kitchen or replace your roof? Maybe you want to play golf every day or stay home with your hobbies. Write down all your goals, both immediate and future.

2. What is your emotional attitude toward your money? Imagine yourself investing part of your retirement fund in stocks. As you may know, stocks fluctuate in value. Let's say the stocks you invested in are moving downward. Do you:

   a. Anxiously check the newspaper every day for stock values? Does the decline of the stock cause you to lose sleep?
   b. Understand that this was a risk you decided to take and you accept the consequences?

It is *your* job to know the answers to these two questions. It will be your advisor's job to tell you whether you can meet your retirement goals given your expenses, your assets and income, and your emotional makeup.

3. Before starting the interview process, become knowledgeable of current interest rates from banks, CDs, money market funds, and the current five-year CD rate. You can find this information in the business section of the newspaper, at your bank, or from any brokerage firm. You will want to write this information down and take it with you to the interviews for comparison.

4. How do you find a financial advisor? What firms should you go to? You can ask friends or relatives whose opinions you respect if they know of and can recommend anyone. Or you can call the human resources department where you worked and ask if they have the name of an advisor whom other retirees use and are happy with. The Institute of Certified Financial Planners in Denver has a list of certified financial planners in your area. The International Association of Financial Planners or the Investment Counsel Association of America can also give you the name of an advisor in your area. These will be independent registered investment advisors (see Resources). You can also call those brokerage firms whose names you recognize from TV or newspaper advertisements and interview brokers with the guidelines we provide.

5. If you call a brokerage firm you have selected on your own, as Anita did, make sure the firm you deal with is a member of the National Association of Securities Dealers (NASD) as well as the Securities Investor Protection Corporation (SICP). Ask to speak with the office manager. Tell the manager that you are retired and want an advisor who has been in the industry at least ten years and specializes in retirement planning. This way you know they have dealt with different economic environments and should understand your needs. Apply the criteria of length of service and specialization to any personal recommendations you receive as well. Do not just walk into a brokerage firm and ask for a broker. If you do, you may be assigned to the new kid on the block with little or no experience.

6. You will need to bring the following financial information to the interview: recent tax returns, Social Security estimates, an idea of monthly expenses, and any sources of present and future income with accompanying statements that show where your money is located.

If you do not know your Social Security estimate, call 800-772-1213 and ask for the questionnaire "Personal Earnings and Benefit Estimate Statement." It will take four to six weeks to receive your estimate after you return the questionnaire, so start early. **The form in Chapter Six, "Early Retirement," will help you calculate your monthly expenses.**

Now you are prepared to go out and interview financial advisors. These interviews should be at no cost to you.

THE INTERVIEW PROCESS

Interview at least one person at three different firms, including any of the recommendations you may have received. Apply these guidelines at each interview. Even personal recommendations need to meet the following standards.

1. If you are a couple, both partners should be present for the interview. It is important that both individuals feel comfortable with the advisor ultimately selected. This is especially important for women, since statistics reveal they generally outlive their male counterparts.

2. Check whether the advisor has a title after his or

her name. If you use someone from a major brokerage firm, the titles, in ascending order of importance, of associate vice president—investments, vice president—investments, senior vice president—investments, or first vice president—investments indicate the advisor's earning power and how long he or she has been in the business. Titles such as account executive, financial advisor, or financial consultant/planner indicate the new kids on the block and show that a certain production level has not yet been achieved for the firm. *Look for at least an associate vice president—investments* credential. Titles can be found on business cards. Remember, *it is only one of the criteria to look for.* Whether the individual is with a major firm or not, there are other things to consider:

3. Is he or she a certified financial planner? If so, it will say so on his or her business card, or you may see a certificate in that person's office, or ask directly. This indicates two years of study, extensive tests, and a minimum of thirty hours of continuing education each year to keep up to date. This designation is highly desirable.

4. Ask how long he or she has been with this firm. It should be a minimum of ten years. If not, ask how many prior companies the person has worked for. Look for an answer of no more than two. Then ask how long he or she stayed at each. An answer of no less than five years at the most recent firm is preferable. This is a powerful clue to stability. If the person has been at many firms for brief durations, it is probably best to find someone else.

5. Meet the advisor in his or her office. **Observe the surroundings.** Is the person organized? Take note of personal appearance.

6. The financial advisor should ask about your goals

during the interview process. If they don't ask, they may care more about what they can *get* from you (commissions) than what they can *do* for you (investments). During the interview, be sure to disclose all your financial information: your goals and requirements, taxes, monthly expenses, Social Security, and other sources of income. *Make your emotional attitude toward money perfectly clear.* Accurate planning requires complete information and assessment.

7. Ask the advisors you are interviewing how they make their money. For your general information, there are three ways a broker/financial advisor makes money: commission only; fee plus commission; or fee only. Fee-only financial planners can charge dearly for an original plan (some work on an hourly basis). However, they are generally more impartial and likely to give better advice. Fee-plus-commission-basis planners charge a small up-front fee for the plan and receive commissions on the investments made. A commission-only advisor makes money only when he or she sells or buys on your account.

Understand those commission rates. Generally they are consistent from one full-service brokerage firm to another. You can ask your advisor-to-be if there is a discount commission available from the firm. Sometimes they are willing to discount, especially for large quantities of stock. Remember, when commissions are involved, planners can steer you toward high-commission investments that will be beneficial to them but not necessarily to you, which is why I favor fee-only planners or the following.

8. A popular alternative is the **registered investment advisor** (RIA). When such advisors manage your money, they receive a fixed percentage of the portfolio as their fee. This can be ¼ percent to 2 percent of the amount of money they have under management for you. *Fees should be paid on a quarterly basis and are not to be taken up front.*

These people do not participate in commissions and are in the unique position of being on the same side of the fence as you. The more money they make for you, the more money they make for themselves. Let's say your RIA is charging you 1 percent to manage your portfolio, which is worth $200,000. The advisor should collect those fees on a quarterly basis based on the value of your portfolio *at that time.* Let's look at this example for the first year: During the first quarter, the portfolio is worth $200,000 (you are just starting out). The advisor receives $500, or ¼ percent of $200,000. By the second quarter, the portfolio is now worth $250,000. He or she receives $625. The third quarter sees a major decline, to $100,000. The advisor will receive only $250. At the end of the fourth quarter your portfolio is back up to $150,000, so the advisor gets $375. Added together, this amounts to $1,750 in fees based on the performance and value of the portfolio at each quarter. If you had given the advisor his or her annual fee up front—$2,000 based on the initial portfolio value—you would have overpaid by $250 in the first year.

Most RIAs do not partake in commissions, but that does not mean there is no cost to you to buy or sell these investments. Because of this, you want an advisor who will hold your funds at a discount brokerage house such as Charles Schwab or Fidelity, so it will cost you less. It also benefits the advisor to do so because if you spend a lot of money on commissions, there will be less in your account to base his or her fees on. RIAs also tend to purchase investments that are commission-free, such as no-load mutual funds, for the same reason. When they purchase stocks at a discount brokerage house, the cost can be 75 percent to 90 percent less than what a full-service firm charges. Your RIA can hold an account at a full-service firm and have made a deal to receive a discounted rate. Make sure to ask. Many RIAs require a minimum amount to open an account, starting at $50,000 to $100,000, with the majority around $250,000.

Wrap Accounts. For purposes of paying commissions, beware of what is referred to as a wrap account. This is when you go to a full-service brokerage firm and your broker suggests that you *put your account under management* with a registered investment advisor. The RIA makes the decisions about what to buy and sell and calls the broker to make the trade. Under these circumstances you may not be charged commissions, but the 2 percent to 3 percent annual fee you are charged will include the commissions. If you use common sense, you can secure a registered investment advisor directly and eliminate the middleman.

The contract with an RIA. Read the contract carefully. It should include the fee payment schedule. Remember, we recommend quarterly payments. Make sure you have the right to fire your advisor anytime you want. If you ever become unhappy with his or her performance, you can simply change your advisor and the funds can remain at the same discount brokerage firm. The RIA can also terminate the contract. Make certain, however, that the fees are prorated under these circumstances. You don't want to pay for services you don't continue to receive. Does the contract state when the termination goes into effect? It should not take more than thirty days to sever your relationship with your advisor.

Your statements with an RIA. Never make a check payable to an RIA, or any advisor, for that matter. Make sure your funds are placed in a firm where the RIA has the right to instruct what to sell and buy, but never to withdraw funds. You should receive a minimum of quarterly updates from your RIA along with monthly statements from the brokerage firm.

As we continue, the following information pertains to *any and all* financial advisors you may interview, including registered investment advisors.

9. The interview process may take one or two meetings before you make a determination. At the first meeting, the advisor gathers information. The second meeting is usually a presentation of a portfolio for you. Some advisors will be able to do both at one meeting.

Once the advisor has shown you what he or she can do with your money, there should also be an explanation of how this portfolio will meet your retirement goals and match your money/emotion ratio. Compare the return the advisor says he or she can make for you with the rates of the five-year CD (remember, you wrote this information down). Is there a difference? If not, you may be better off investing in a five-year CD yourself—no risk, no commissions. If it is more than 4 percent higher, you need to question the safety of the investments being offered. Ask the advisor what the chances are of losing any of your investment. If you don't feel comfortable with the advisor's answers, this is not the advisor for you. Look for someone else. If everything seems right, ask to have *all* the information regarding the return and safety of the investments in writing on company stationery.

10. Now that you have interviewed using the process we discussed, you must **verify all the information** the advisor, broker, or financial planner gives you for accuracy and to make sure they are not hiding any information they do not want you to know, such as

TIP:

Look for a registered investment advisor who charges no more than 2 percent annually, including costs to buy or sell any of your investments.

TIP:

When interviewing an advisor, ask for ten references (with addresses and phone numbers). Make sure you call everyone on the list to see how they have done.

disciplinary actions or criminal investigations. To obtain verification, you can call:

NASD/Public Disclosure Program
Tel.: 800-289-9999

Call for a form. There is a $30 charge for a report.

11. Always read documents first—in their entirety— before signing them. Don't be rushed. Take the documents home to read. Do you and your spouse or significant other understand the investments the advisor recommends? Jot down points that need clarification and ask questions about *anything* you don't understand.

OPENING AN ACCOUNT

Once you understand what is going to be done with your money, and have chosen a particular advisor, it is time to open an investment account. The following guidelines will prevent you from making the same mistakes as Anita:

1. Never sign blank documents. Only sign documents when all your personal and financial information is correct. Brokerage firms are set up to protect the investor. The office manager monitors advisor activity to make sure advisors are trading client funds according to the risk factors indicated by the client's financial profile and wishes. This is known as the "know your customer rule." The firm's only way to monitor its advisors is by the financial information you provide and sign. In Anita's case, she had only $10,000 when she opened the account with Patti. But she signed blank documents enabling her advisor to falsify the information.

2. Get everything in writing on the company's letterhead —not on scraps of notepaper. Don't accept verbal promises. Don't sign anything until you have everything you want or have heard *in writing*. Keep these in a file.

3. Signing a "discretionary" account form that allows anyone other than an RIA to do anything he or she wants with your money is not advisable. This is particularly true if your advisor works on a commission basis.

4. Make sure you request and receive copies of *all* original documents. Keep these in your file. In case anything goes wrong and you need to make a formal complaint, all the information you need will be on hand.

MONITORING YOUR ACCOUNT

For an advisor, getting your account is one thing, keeping it is another. Even after you have selected an advisor, continue to monitor his or her performance monthly.

1. It is to your benefit to **learn how to read your statements** and know what is being done with your money. Your advisor should offer to teach you. Don't be afraid to ask. Don't take "no" for an answer or let the matter slide. If your advisor is resistant, you can always transfer your account to another advisor or institution.

2. Compare your statements from month to month. **Be sure you know which line is the one that tells you how much you are worth!** Is your account total going up or down? If it is going down, find out why immediately.

3. Be aware that *every time* a trade is made on your behalf, **you must be called beforehand for your approval** (unless you have signed a discretionary account form with a registered investment advisor). Nothing should ever be bought or sold without your explicit approval. Also note that each time there is a trade in your account, a confirmation slip will be sent to you. **If you get slips in the mail that you are not expecting** or don't understand, **call** the advisor (or the office manager) and **question** what is being done with your account. **A lot of mail may mean a lot of trading**!

4. If you don't understand the ramifications of what your advisor wants to do with your money on a buy or sell, **don't do it!** The old adage of "better safe than sorry" fits the situation.

5. At least once a year, calculate the return you are getting on your funds. Use this formula if you have not withdrawn any money from the account for that year:

(year-end balance) − (beginning-year balance) =
sum ÷ (beginning year balance) = % return

For example, $50,000 − $40,000 = $10,000 ÷
$40,000 = .25 or 25% return

If you don't know how to calculate your return, or need to verify your calculations, ask your advisor. Again, it is best to have the information put on the company's letterhead for your review and records.

6. Pay attention to all information you receive. Ignoring information may create future problems. It might be a mistake you cannot afford to make.

7. Most good investments are held for a number of years, not bought and sold within months. (Anita's advisor bought and sold one mutual fund in just one day.) Keep track of how often investments are bought and then sold. Anything held less than six months to a year on a frequent basis (unless done by a RIA) may be a warning signal that commissions are more important to the advisor than your financial growth. If this happens, talk to the firm's manager or seek another professional opinion.

These are the recommended guidelines for finding and monitoring a financial advisor. If you already have an advisor, check him or her against these criteria and continue to employ these guidelines throughout your relationship. If at any time you feel something is not right with your account, or you feel you have lost any of your money unfairly, don't hesitate to speak with the office manager at the brokerage firm and explain what happened. If he or she says that nothing can be done or you have no rights, double-check the accuracy of the response by calling the NASD.

This is *your* money. Always stay involved and knowledgeable about it. There is a difference between letting someone invest your money and letting someone control your money. What happens to it will directly affect the quality of your retirement. Remember, Anita's outcome doesn't have to be yours.

chapter 2

Avoiding Estates of Confusion: Trusts vs. Wills

This old house has been in our family for five generations. It was always assumed that I would live out my years here, surrounded by my heritage. I could sell the house for money to live on . . . *but how do you sell your heritage?*

Marcia's Story

I'm sixty-four now and I still have such fond memories of growing up in Connecticut. My parents' house sat on one and a half acres of land that were dark green and fragrant in the summer and picture-postcard white in winter. The house was one hundred fifty years old then, and every room was filled with precious antiques, each reminding us of a story about some family member. When I grew up, I moved away and bought a house in Bolinas, California, never losing sight of returning one day.

It was when Father died and Mother became ill that I rented my house in Bolinas and moved back to take care of her. When she finally died, I knew I wanted to remain in the house. Because I was an only child, it was always assumed that everything would be mine someday. I would live out my years there surrounded by our family heritage. It had given Mother such comfort knowing I would be financially secure. Of course, no one ever thought there was anything to worry about. Mother and Father had made out a will. They thought they had done everything they were supposed to do to protect me. It never dawned on them that with only a will I would have to pay hundreds of thousands of dollars to keep what was really already mine.

The process of settling the estate began right after Mother's death. We had realtors appraise the house and land and submitted that figure to the IRS. Months later the IRS came back and assigned a considerably higher value. They appraised the land and the house, along with the antiques, at $1.2 million. I never thought the property was worth anywhere near what they indicated. I challenged the IRS appraisal, but they stuck firm.

The IRS based their estimate on recorded sales of surrounding homes, most of which were much newer or had been modernized. They never even took a look at my house. The last time our house was renovated was in the 1940s. I cook in a 1940s kitchen. The house has a sixty-watt electrical system and only one bathroom. Goodness, there's still a dirt basement! So when they told me I now owed $235,000 in estate taxes, I nearly fainted. Where was I going to get that much money? Mother just had the house and the property. There was no cash to speak of. The IRS already allowed a six-month extension to pay the money. They said I would not have to pay a penalty, but I would have to pay interest. I didn't know what I was going to do! Now we were only a few months away from this deadline, and the IRS was not going to allow us any more extensions.

I talked to just about everyone I could think of, looking for help. One suggestion was to divide the land into lots and sell off some of the lots to pay the tax, but it would have taken time to do that and I didn't have much time left. So my lawyer suggested that my only alternative was to take out a bank loan. At that time, with interest rates so high, the best I could do was a 12 percent loan that had to be paid back in two years. *Because I had no income, I had to borrow an extra $100,000 to pay the payments on the loan.* The bank used the house and the land as collateral. I knew that if I took this loan, I would definitely have to sell off the land to pay back the bank within the next two years or I would lose everything. What choice did I have? So I borrowed $335,000.

As soon as the loan cleared and the IRS was paid, I began the process of subdividing the land into six lots and trying to sell them myself. By the time I put them on the market, property values began to drop dramatically and the lots just weren't selling for my asking price of $110,000 each. The highest anyone was willing to pay was $65,000 per lot. That was $45,000 less per lot than the IRS valued them at and I paid estate taxes on. I felt so pressured because my two years on the loan were almost up. I had to sell quickly to pay back the loan, so I took the offers, leaving me little to live on. Since it was obvious that I was going to need money, I sold my house in Bolinas.

Today I receive about $4,000 a year in interest from the money I received when I sold my home in California, along with my Social Security of $8,000 a year, giving me a total of $12,000 a year to live on. My expenses for my health insurance alone are $4,000 a year. The property taxes are $5,000 a year. That leaves me only $3,000 to pay for everything else—food, electricity, telephone, clothes, and such. I always have a sense of anxiety about spending any money.

But the saddest thing of all is that I never had a chance to grieve over my mother's death.

Discussion

M ARCIA'S MOTHER never had any idea that there would be problems, because everything passed to her quickly and smoothly when her husband died. There was never any mention of estate tax being owed—no taxes, no lawyers, no court procedures or fees. There was no reason for her to think that this wouldn't be the case for her daughter as well.

The primary reason that everything went so smoothly for Marcia's mother was that the house and land they owned were held in joint tenancy with right of survivorship, not because they had a will. By holding title in joint tenancy, which is how most married couples own their property, when one person dies, the entire property automatically becomes the surviving person's property.

There was never any mention of estate tax because one spouse can leave the other spouse any amount of money and property completely free of all estate tax. It is when the surviving spouse dies and leaves the estate (property and money) to their children or other heirs that estate tax, or other fees, could be suddenly owed, as was the case with Marcia.

There is a way to avoid the problems that Marcia encountered: While both her parents were alive they should have done estate tax planning and set up a marital trust, also known as an A-B trust. Before we actually discuss some of the different trusts and how they work, it is important to understand the workings of a will and why it may not be the best way to leave assets to your beneficiaries.

This discussion, remember, is based on the assumption that when the husband and the wife have both died, their property then passes on to their beneficiaries.

THE WILL

A will is a legal document that simply states your intentions and identifies to whom you wish to pass your money and property (your estate) when you die. To make the transfer from your name to your beneficiaries' names, they will have to go to court and get a court order by a judge. The court order gives your beneficiaries the legal authority to transfer ownership of the property and bank accounts from your name (the deceased) to theirs. Nothing officially belongs to them until this procedure is completed. This procedure is known as probate.

PROBATING A WILL

Unfortunately, to get the court order, your beneficiaries may have to pay court fees; attorney fees; and, in some cases, executor fees. In many states these fees are set by law. For example, let's say you live in California and all you have to your name is a home worth $300,000. You thoughtfully draw up a will to leave this home to your children. Upon your death, however, the will has to be "probated." The fees to probate a $300,000 estate will be at least $14,300 in California and must be *paid at the time the court order is entered.* It does not matter how much you still owe on the house; if it is worth $300,000, that will be the amount probated. An additional $1,000 or so must be paid *up front* as court costs. This includes (approximately) $180 in probate filing fees, $200 for a public notice of death, 1% of the appraised value of the estate for a court appointed referee, and $300 in certification and recording fees. If your children do not have this kind of money, they will either have to take out a loan or sell the house just to pay the probate fees.

It doesn't matter which state you live in; your will will be probated. Not all states, however, have statutory fees. In Marcia's case, even though she had to pay estate taxes due to the value of the property, she did not have to pay statutory probate fees because the state of Connecticut does not require them. But she did pay a required fee to her lawyer to do the probate work. If Marcia's mother had lived in New York, she could have owed an extra $39,000 for probate fees on top of the $235,000 she owed in estate tax. Note that statutory fees for attorneys and executors can be waived, or one can act as one's own attorney.

Regardless of whether you live in a state that requires fees or not, there are other problems that arise when dealing with wills and probate.

The comparison of fees in the following chart uses California and New York as examples because they are the two states with the highest rates. California shows the combined fee for executor and lawyer, each getting half. New York, on the other hand, shows only the fee for the executor; lawyer's fees are extra. None of these figures includes filing fees, publication fees, or fees for a probate referee to appraise the estate, if needed.

Estate Size	California Combined Executor/Lawyer fee	New York Executor fee (Lawyer fees are extra)
$ 100,000	$ 6,300	$ 5,000
200,000	10,300	9,000
300,000	14,300	13,000
400,000	18,300	16,000
500,000	22,300	19,000
600,000	26,300	22,000
750,000	32,300	26,500
1,000,000	42,300	34,000
1,200,000	46,300	39,000

PROBLEMS WITH PROBATE

THE ISSUE OF PUBLIC RECORD

Because a will must be probated and therefore has to go through the court system, everything you identify to leave to your beneficiaries in the will becomes a matter of public record. This means that *anyone* can go to the court records and discover the value of your estate. This may not sound terrible, but there are swindlers just waiting to prey on the vulnerable. There is the case of a stockbroker who checked court records monthly. If he saw a case where the husband died and left a sizable stock portfolio, he immediately called the widow to say that her husband had asked him to help manage the portfolio. He was shrewd and convincing; he would name some of the stocks in the portfolio so the widow would think he was telling the truth. Before anyone knew what was happening, she had handed over her entire portfolio to him.

Furthermore, as part of the probate proceedings, you are required by law to place a notice of the death in the newspapers. The issue of privacy usually rears its head when some unfriendly relative or disgruntled business associate happens to see the notice and wants to make a claim to some of your money; all they have to do is to "contest" the will. The estate could easily be tied up for many years to come. Unfortunately, this happens all too often.

A CONSERVATORSHIP

A will does not deal with issues such as the possibility of conservatorship; this needs to be addressed while you are alive. It only instructs the court as to whom you want to get your property, money, and valuables upon your death. Should you develop Alzheimer's disease or become unable to deal with your affairs, a conservatorship may have to be established. It is a most unpleasant and expensive procedure to have to go to court to have someone declared incompetent in order to gain conservatorship over that person's affairs.

THE ISSUE OF GUARDIANSHIP

A will cannot legally appoint someone as a guardian for a child. Again, it merely states your wishes. So your son Jonathan, who is thirty-five, and his wife, Tracy, just had their first child—your first grandchild. They decide it is time to have a will drawn up indicating that if anything happened to them, you will become guardian of the child. If something were to happen to Jonathan and Tracy, their will would still have to be probated and *the court would establish a probate guardianship*. The court can decide that it is in the best interest of the child not to appoint you the guardian and select someone else. The court even has the right to control all funds your grandchild inherits until he or she turns eighteen.

INCOME TAX

A point that is always overlooked is that during the probate period, your beneficiaries may be required to file a separate income tax return for the probate estate. If it takes two years to settle your estate, which is not uncommon, your beneficiaries may have to file (and pay) income taxes for the estate during that entire time.

ESTATE TAX

The biggest financial drawback of a simple will is that it does not alleviate the estate tax burden. No one in their right mind would ever consider making the IRS one of the main beneficiaries of their money. But if you do not take the proper planning steps now, that is exactly what you could be doing. It seems that the old adage "Where there is a will there is a way" should perhaps read, "Where there is only a will *you are going to pay!*"

THE TRUST

If you want to avoid the problems that having only a will or not having a will creates, consider having a trust. The following portion of this discussion will give you a basic understanding of some of the different trusts and how they can benefit you. Since I am not a lawyer, the information presented here is an interview with my associate Janet Dobrovolny, an attorney who is an expert in the area of trusts. I asked her questions I thought would be most helpful to you. Let's begin with a few key terms you will need to know:

Revocable Trust or Living Trust. The document, as it is generally referred to.

Trustor. The person who creates the trust, who owns the property that will be put in the trust. That would be you. When setting up a trust with a partner or a spouse, you would be known as trustors.

Trustee. The person you designate to make all the decisions about the money and property in the trust. Ninety-nine percent of the time this will be you. Again, if you and your partner or spouse are designated together, then you are known as cotrustees. An institution can also be named as a trustee, if you wish.

Successor Trustee. The person, or people, you designate to manage your trust if something happens to you.

Beneficiary or beneficiaries. The person or people who will receive the assets of the trust upon your death.

The following questions and answers essentially show you how a trust works.

What is a trust?

A trust is a device that allows you to transfer legal title of your property to another person (or to yourself as trustee) to hold for the benefit of yet another person (beneficiary) in the cheapest and most effective way. Consider the oldest known history of a trust. Land was given to medieval knights for their service in battle. As long as they served the king, they kept the land. But battle-worn knights who no longer wanted to fight began to pay the king a fee for the land instead of paying service. They also began to discover that they could give title to the land to the Church, which paid no fees to the king, while remaining on the land for as long as generations. The knights trusted the Church to continue to allow them to use the land. So the knights used the land, the Church held the title, and the king got cut out. And here we are doing the same thing today—transferring title into a trust (Church) and avoiding any fees (king).

What is the difference between a trust and a will?

Will: The primary difference is that the provisions of a will can be carried out only by a court order—a lengthy and expensive process. As was mentioned before, when your estate is probated, you will have to file a separate income tax return for the estate, as well as disclose private financial information for public record.

Trust: A trust gives the trustee the legal authority to distribute assets immediately to the beneficiaries based on the terms of the trust. *No court is involved*. No public notice of death is required as it is with a will. All that is required is a death certificate and a trust document that describes how things are to be distributed through the trust. Because a trust bypasses the court system, or probate, there are no fees, and there is no public record of the value of your estate, protecting your privacy.

How is a will prepared?

A document is drawn up in accordance with your wishes. It is in a certain format, is signed by you, and is witnessed by two or three people. Now you have a will.

How is a trust prepared?

You do almost exactly the same thing—a document is drawn up according to a particular format. You sign it, and your signature is notarized. The titles to all your properties are then transferred into the trust. So your deed, for example, will no longer read "Suze Orman," it will read "Suze Orman, trustee for the Suze Orman Trust."

Who should have a trust?

Almost everyone should have a trust, especially those who live in states where there are statutory probate fees. Setting up a trust is beneficial if you own a home or real estate. Even if you live in a state where there aren't statutory probate fees, a trust will usually cost less than the lawyer's fee and court fees for the probate proceedings. The court and the lawyers benefit if you do not have a trust. Even the federal government— and, in some cases, the state—benefit when estate taxes are due.

Who shouldn't have a trust?

People who can pass property and assets by a probate affidavit* or other informal procedure should not have a trust. For those who are in the midst of applying for Medicaid or if there is a strong possibility, because of age and financial conditions, that such assistance may be needed in the near future, a trust is not recommended as well. If you have Medicaid and already have a trust, be sure to consult an expert in this area about financial ramifications. (Remember, Medicaid is assistance for the needy. That generally indicates financial hardship, which we are trying to help you avoid!) So the answer to our question is that very, very few people should not have a trust.

What's the point of a will, you ask?

There really isn't much point. You can prepare a will as a backup in order to pass on items such as jewelry and furniture that don't have a legal title and to express your wishes regarding disposition of your remains and memorial services.

TIP:

*A probate affidavit is a legal form stating that assets are under a certain designated value. When beneficiaries present the sworn document to a title holder, such as a bank or mutual fund company, showing entitlement, the title holder may then legally transfer the assets to the beneficiary without a court order. This designated value may vary from state to state, according to each state's probate requirements.

Why don't more people have a trust?

People don't understand what a trust is and how it works because most general practice attorneys are not well versed in trusts and don't explain them in an understandable way. Traditionally, too, the terms "trust" and "estate" have always been associated with the very rich. That just isn't so anymore.

Do you need a lawyer to draw up a trust, or can you get a trust "form" at a stationery store or from a book or use your financial planner?

If all you have is a house, Nolo Press* has a great do-it-yourself book available. If you have more than just a house, or you aren't the type who will take the time to read the book, it would be wise to consult with a lawyer who specializes in trusts.

Why do some lawyers tell you that you do not need a trust unless you have a really large estate?

Here's a little quiz: If you were a lawyer, would you rather make $750 to $2,000 to draw up a trust, or thousands and thousands of dollars to probate a will? Even an estate with a value of $100,000 will earn a lawyer $3,150 and the executor $3,150 in fees. Basically, you and your heirs could lose if you don't have a trust. Everyone else wins. Do you get it yet? The majority of people are better off with a trust.

Plan Your Estate With a Living Trust, by Denis Clifford. Nolo Press, 950 Parker Street, Berkeley, CA 94710. Orderline: 1-800-992-6656. Credit cards are accepted.

GET IT IN WRITING

I cannot stress this enough: If you go to a lawyer who says you need only a will, I want you to ask that lawyer these three questions:

1. If a basic trust is relevant to our circumstances, how much will it cost to have one prepared?

2. If we (you and your spouse) have only a will and we both die right now, how much will it cost our beneficiaries in probate and legal fees to transfer everything we own?

3. If we have a living trust and, again, suppose we both die right now, how much will it cost our beneficiaries to obtain everything we want to pass on to them?

Now all you have to do is compare the two costs: setting up a trust versus drawing up a will. In both cases, make sure to add in any fees that would be charged to your beneficiaries after your death. So what's the bottom line? If it is more cost-effective to have a trust, maybe you should seek another lawyer, one who has your best interests at heart. On the other hand, you might want to stay with him if he can clearly explain why you do not need a trust at this point. But be sure *to review this procedure every few years.* You never know when your situation or the laws will change, making it more beneficial for you to have a trust.

Most importantly, don't let someone talk you out of something that may save a considerable amount of money. Ask to have these amounts put in writing on his letterhead with an explanation of what the fees are for. If the lawyer won't do it, and you decide to take this lawyer's advice and things turn out badly, it will be impossible for your beneficiaries to prove that you relied on his advice unless you have it in writing and have it updated regularly.

Can a revocable living trust be changed at any time?

Yes. It can be amended easily at any time although it may cost a nominal fee. This is why it is referred to as a revocable living trust.

What is the main purpose of a revocable living trust?

The purpose is to avoid the probate procedure! The reason that a trust bypasses probate is that you have taken the steps, while you are alive, to transfer assets from your name as an individual into the separate entity of the trust. When you die, the trust doesn't die. It simply appoints the successor trustee, whom you have selected, and gives that person the legal authority to sign over the contents of the trust to whomever you have designated as your beneficiary. The successor trustee and the beneficiary can be the same person.

Do you give up any control when you place your assets into a trust?

Absolutely none. It's like creating a corporation where you are the sole stockholder, the director, and the president. No one else makes any management decisions or has control over anything that goes on in that corporation but you. The trust works in exactly the same way. You create it, set forth the terms, and have full management and control over all the assets that are in it.

Why do people think that once they have a trust they can't make any changes?

They haven't learned about the differences between a revocable, or changeable trust, and an irrevocable trust. Actually, a trust is easier to amend than a will because it doesn't require two witnesses to institute the change. Some attorneys will provide you with an easy-to-follow form that allows you to prepare the amendment yourself.

Is there a difference between a checking and savings account in one's individual name and in the trust name?

The only difference you might encounter is with the $100,000 FDIC protection. Banks explain that if you and your spouse each have $100,000 in savings, each is protected to the full amount. They may also say that if you combine the money under a trust, they will only insure you up to $100,000. Some banks, however, will still allow both to maintain the $100,000 limits. Check with your bank.

Will the bank refinance your home while it is in a trust?

This depends on the bank. Some may want you to transfer the house back into your individual name to sign the loan. Afterward, you can transfer it right back into the trust. This is not a problem, and any title company should do this as part of the refinancing. Your attorney can transfer the house back into the trust for as little as $25 to $50.

How important is the trustee in the trust?

That's like asking how important chocolate is in a chocolate milkshake. The trustee is the person who makes all the decisions about your money while you are alive. Certainly if you are capable of setting up a trust and handling your own money, the trustee should be you. However, if you choose not to be trustee of your trust because you are incapacitated, the word "trust" becomes more significant. The appointed trustee should be someone you trust completely to make necessary decisions on your behalf and to have your best interests at heart.

Is there an advantage to appointing someone else to act as trustee of your trust while you are alive and competent?

Very rarely.

Should there be only one trustee, or can there be more than one trustee?

You can have one trustee or cotrustees. With cotrustees, all have to agree and sign on everything unless you specify otherwise. Having one or more trustees will depend on your specific family characteristics and needs. It is a completely personal decision. Your attorney should discuss all alternatives with you, explain each option, and point out the advantages and disadvantages of each so you can decide knowledgeably. Ultimately you must make the final decisions.

Can a trust benefit me while I am alive? Or can it benefit only my beneficiaries, after my death?

A trust is as much for its creators as it is for its beneficiaries. In the case of incapacity, that a trust exists can be invaluable. Here's an example: You and your spouse own a house in joint tenancy. Your spouse has a severe stroke and becomes incapacitated: he is unable to work, sign his name, or even recognize you. Because of the reduction in family income, or because a move to a one-story home would make caring for your spouse easier, you decide to sell your house. May you do so? The answer is no: Since you both own it, both of your signatures must be on the sales agreement.

Is there anything you can do? In order to sell, you will have to go to court, have your spouse declared incompetent, and have a conservator assigned. This could cost you several thousand dollars. Furthermore, after you sell the home, you will be forced to seek the court's permission any time you wish to make use of any of your spouse's share of the proceeds.

If, on the other hand, the two of you had created

a trust with an incapacity clause that authorizes a co-trustee or successor trustee to sign for your incapacitated spouse, you will be able to bypass the courts and avoid fees.

Does a trust file a separate income tax return?

Not if it's a revocable trust and the trustor is also a trustee. For IRS purposes, no completed transfer has occurred. It's not a real entity for tax purposes, so you just file your regular tax returns.

How often should someone update a trust?

If it is a simple revocable living trust and no estate tax planning has been incorporated in the trust, you probably won't have to make any updates in the trust unless there is an unexpected death in the family or a major change of circumstance or relationship.

Where should a trust document be kept?

Keep the document in your home where it is easily accessible to the successor trustee, or in a safe deposit box in the name of the trust. Be sure to tell the successor trustee where it is and how to get it in the event of your death.

As you have seen, a revocable living trust saves you time, public scrutiny, and money. For many of you, though, the most important feature of a trust may be the savings of thousands of dollars in estate tax. In Marcia's situation, the reason she was left in such a terrible state was that she owed estate taxes. For this a different kind of trust is needed.

ESTATE TAX

Estate tax differs from income tax in that income tax is owed every year on any incoming revenue.

Estate tax is owed on the net value of your estate (if that estate is above a certain value) at the time of

TIPS:

The amount you can pass on to beneficiaries before estate tax is owed increases over the next years as follows:

1998	*$625,000*
1999	*$650,000*
2000–2001	*$675,000*
2002–2003	*$700,000*
2004	*$850,000*
2005	*$950,000*
2006	*$1,000,000*

your death if you leave your assets to any beneficiary other than your spouse. Essentially your estate is made up of everything you own: life insurance proceeds, your IRA, your cars, your jewelry, etc., less any debts you may owe on that property. If your home is worth $200,000 but you still owe $95,000 on your mortgage, only $105,000 would be included in your net estate from that property.

How much can you pass on to beneficiaries before estate tax is owed?

In 1998,* you can give or bequeath $625,000 to your beneficiaries free of gift or estate tax. Any amount over that and your beneficiaries will pay dearly.

How can you reduce estate taxes by gifting?

To reduce estate taxes to beneficiaries, if your estate is larger than the allowable amount, you might want to reduce the size of the estate by gifting money. In Chapter Three we discuss the allowable $10,000 per person per year. But did you know that you can pay college tuition directly to a college in any amount, even if it exceeds $10,000, and not pay any additional gift tax? For instance, you can gift a grandchild, or anyone else, $10,000 a year plus pay her annual college tuition, which can be sizable, and reduce the size of your estate.

HOW TO AVOID ESTATE TAX

By setting up an A-B trust while both partners are alive you can double the amount of money you can leave to your beneficiaries free of estate taxes. Getting back to Marcia's parents: Had they simply set up an A-B trust, everything would have been left to Marcia without a penny owed on the estate. She could have kept her house in Bolinas and all the money from the sale of the lots to generate income for her to live a comfortable lifestyle. Instead, she paid $235,000.

How does an A-B trust differ from a revocable living trust?

A revocable living trust is simply a vehicle that helps you transfer legal title quickly and effectively. It eliminates probate fees, court costs, time delays, etc., but it is not relevant to reducing any estate tax liability.

An A-B trust for spouses was devised to reduce your estate tax liability. It can currently shelter up to $1.25 million. An A-B trust can be created as part of a revocable trust or part of a will as a testamentary trust.* However, a testamentary trust created in a will still has to be probated and, therefore, is not advisable.

Here is how it would have worked for Marcia's parents:

When Marcia's father died, his "half" of the $1.2 million estate, or $600,000, would have passed into the "A" portion of the trust rather than directly to Marcia's mother. Marcia's mother would be the trustee of that trust. She would receive all the income the trust produced. If Marcia's mother used up all her "half" of the funds (the "B" part of the trust), she could take as much of the principal from the "A" portion of the trust as needed.* For the surviving spouse, the reality of the A-B trust should be that money is handled no differently than if it wasn't in the trust. When the mother dies, the A and B portions both go to Marcia.

Here is where the difference comes into play. Because money or property went directly from Marcia's father into the trust, it never became a part of her mother's estate. Any money coming to Marcia from the "A" portion of the trust had the father's credit applied to it. Her mother's half of the estate, also valued at $600,000, was allowed to pass down to Marcia using her mother's credit. In this way Marcia received $600,000 from each parent. If the father had left his $600,000 outright to the mother, no tax would be due at the time of his death because there is no tax between spouses. However, at the time her mother died, the entire $1.2 million would be in her estate and she could pass only $625,000, estate-tax-free, with the result that Marcia would owe $230,000 in estate tax. The A-B trust prevents this from happening. The end result is that Marcia would have received all $1.2 million in property and owed *nothing* in estate taxes had her parents created an A-B trust. This is standard estate planning but requires that both partners be alive at the time the plan is created.

You may feel this is not worth investigating because your net estate is not $625,000, but you must make sure you total *everything* you own—the house, life insurance, pensions, retirement plans with death benefits, all proceeds payable at your death, all investments, art collections, antiques, everything. You may be surprised if you own a home how quickly everything adds up. Marcia was surprised to learn that the house and the land were valued so highly. If you have done a realistic calculation and you still feel your estate value falls short of the $625,000 figure, beware of any reduction in the estate tax exemption. If the law changes, be ready to establish and A-B trust.

Is an A-B trust just for a husband and wife?

Unmarried couples, same-sex couples, or just two friends can get the same benefit up to $1.25 million by establishing separate trusts, which remain intact until both partners have died.

Who benefits from an A-B trust?

Ultimately it is your children, or other named beneficiaries, who will reap the benefit of this trust. Remember, a deceased husband or wife can pass assets to the other without any estate tax at all. This is known as the unlimited marital deduction.

Guidelines

Trusts are a sound defense strategy. But now that you are aware of them, don't march right out and set up a trust with the first lawyer you see! It is important that you choose a lawyer who knows and understands the use of trusts. I have seen many horror stories of people who sought help from an attorney to set up a trust, even paid a lot of money for it, only to discover that the trust had not been funded properly, or they had paid far too much for the service, or worse, that the provisions did not reflect their wishes, or that they were told they only needed a will.

Here are some attorney-shopping guidelines to follow to help avoid mistakes your family cannot afford to make:

FINDING AN ATTORNEY WHO CAN PREPARE A TRUST

There are never guarantees, but you should seek someone who creates trusts and does estate planning exclusively. They should have worked in this field for at least five years.

Ask for references.

I don't know why people have such a hard time asking professionals—whether doctors, lawyers, or stockbrokers—for references, but you should ask for them and make the phone calls. Ask the attorney's clients about the service they received. How much time was

TIP:

Because the trust is created for the benefit of your heirs, or others who will get your property after you are both gone, why not ask them to reimburse you for the cost of setting up the trust? Marcia would have gladly paid $2,500 to save more than $230,000.

spent with them? Was the trust document explained in detail? Did the attorney answer their questions?

Meet and interview each attorney.

Meet with your potential choices in person before you sign with anyone. An attorney should give you a half-hour consultation free of cost. You should feel comfortable in their presence. Remember, this is the person your family will be dealing with when the death of a loved one occurs. You should feel that the attorney answered your questions. Does the attorney intimidate you, or encourage your participation? Trust your inner senses about how you really feel about each person you interview. There are many competent and compassionate trust lawyers out there. Be choosy! You don't want someone who "needs" your business.

Determine community service.

Another factor you might want to consider, although not a stipulation, is whether the attorney is active in the community. People who are service-oriented give to their community as well as to their clients. It's not a bad standard to measure against.

Find out exactly what the fees and services will be.

Get this information up front. Any attorney who answers with "Don't worry about it" or "My fees are standard" without a price attached to the statement, or does not even offer the information, should never be considered. My particular preference is an attorney who bills on a project-by-project basis. In this way, if they misjudge what it costs them to create your trust, they are obliged to complete the work, but it shouldn't cost you any more. When you work with someone who bills on an hourly basis, you are inadvertently encouraging that person to take more time to earn more money. The most common source of client dissatisfaction is receiving a bigger bill for more than they had bargained for. Certainly a lawyer who has performed a significant amount of trust work should be able to quote the job in toto once he or she has established the size of your estate and the type of planning it requires.

What is a good approximate price for a simple trust?

I will use California as an example, since most people can compare their cost of living to that of California. A simple revocable or living trust that takes into consideration one individual, or a couple with one piece of property, a few bank accounts, and not much else, should cost about $750 to $1,000. Never consider a trust that will only cost you a few hundred dollars, unless it is your cousin the trust attorney handling it and you are merely covering expenses. Attorneys who do not charge standard fees for their services usually do not spend adequate time gathering information or explaining the procedure, or are going to leave you to fund the trust, unless you want to pay an additional charge.

The lawyer you select to create your trust should also be able to advise you on estate planning.

A lawyer should look out for your best interests in a number of ways when working on a trust. Subjects such as long-term-care insurance, health care and advance directives, gifting programs, or your charitable inclinations should come up. Look for this type of expanded and detailed service. For example, what would be the point of setting up a trust only to see your assets dwindle from long-term-care costs? *Remember, a revocable trust does not protect your assets. It only bypasses probate.*

WHEN SHOULD PEOPLE SEEK OUT ESTATE TAX PLANNING?

It is hard to say, with possible changes pending, but if you are looking at an estate of $625,000 or more, seek some professional advice.

What is a good approximate price for an A-B trust?
If you have an estate worth $600,000 to $1 million, creating an A-B trust could cost from $1,000 to $2,000, depending on the number of properties that must be transferred into the trust. The more real estate and individual investments you have to transfer into the trust, the more expensive it will be.

WHAT SERVICES DO THE ATTORNEY'S FEES ACTUALLY COVER?

It is important that you know exactly what you are paying the attorney to do. To draw up your trust will not be the bulk of the attorney's work. That is because most trusts start out as boilerplate. This means that the body of the trust, a basic written copy of it, is on the computer and the attorney needs only modify a few sections and create the distribution of assets according to your wishes. So even though this is an essential part of what the attorney has to do, for purposes of the simple trust this is easily and quickly done and not worth the $750 to $1,000 you will be paying. Therefore, the following are additional services your attorney should be providing for you. If not, find another attorney!

The explanation. What does take a long time is an explanation of the documents, what the various words and phrases mean, and making sure you haven't left out any details concerning your assets. A detailed and careful explanation of everything you need to know can take quite a few hours. Not understanding what has been done to set up your trust may allow you inadvertently to do something down the road that could sabotage your own plan. Ask how much time the attorney will take to explain the trust to you. It should be as much time as necessary, usually two to three hours.

Funding the trust. Most importantly, you want to make sure your attorney will be funding the trust for you. This is done by changing the title of your assets from individual name to trust name. The fee you pay a lawyer should include making the necessary document changes for you. It will do you absolutely no good to have trust documents drawn up if your assets are not put into the trust.

The backup will. Your fee should also include drafting a backup will and a durable power of attorney for health care (see Chapter Four).

Here's a quick checklist of the services the attorney should perform:

- drawing up the trust document;
- explaining the trust documents to you in person and in detail (two to five hours);
- transferring all the assets into the trust;
- drafting an updated will and a durable power of attorney for health care.

Find an attorney who will fit these guidelines.

TO FIND AN ATTORNEY

A good place to find an attorney if you do not have one or know of one is The American College of Trust and Estate Counsel. This is a professional association made up of more than 2,600 legal professionals who are extensively versed in estate planning. To receive a list of members in your area you can write to:

> **TIP:**
>
> *Your trust should include provision for determining incapacity so your successor trustee can manage assets for you in case you become incompetent.*

The American College of Trust and Estate Counsel
3415 South Sepulveda Blvd., Suite 460
Los Angeles, CA 90034
Tel: 310-398-1888
Fax: 310-572-7280

Another good resource is available at your library:
The Martindale-Hubbell® Law Directory
or through the Internet:
The Martindale-Hubbell® Lawyer Locator™

Other ideas:

- Always use personal references as your best resource. Check with your place of worship. There may be members of your congregation who can also give you a personal reference.
- If that is not possible you might want to contact the Alzheimer's Association in your area and ask if they know of any good lawyers.
- Also, ask local charities. They may be aware of the work of a good trust lawyer in your area.

Joint Tenancy with Right of Survivorship and Gifting

Shock waves ran through us when we discovered that Dad's will was void and the childhood home we cherished was not ours to inherit.

Carol and Joe's Story

Carol: When Dad remarried a year after Mom died, my brother, Joe, and I stood up for him at the wedding. It was good to see him smile and laugh again because Mom's death had hit him hard. It threw us all off balance and took some time to get back on track, but seeing Dad so miserable made us realize that it was okay for him to remarry if it would make him happy. Life has to go on, you know, so why not make the best of it.

Joe: Dad's new wife, Stephanie, and her three children moved into the house Carol and I grew up in. It's an ample house with timeless architecture and acres of grounds—a great place for kids to grow up. There were still lots of Mom's things in the house, her collections and special touches, but Stephanie is a decorator, so she incorporated them into her own look quite adeptly.

Carol: Stephanie admitted, though, that she wasn't much of a gardener, so I gladly came over every week to take care of Mom's lavish rose garden. It was her pride and joy. No one else was ever allowed to touch her prize-winning roses. She tended those roses the same way she took care of Joe and me when we were youngsters. She would refer to them as her "other children," and to all of us collectively as her "jewels."

Joe: Everything went along just fine for years until Dad succumbed to a heart attack. We knew in advance that he had prepared his will to allow Stephanie to live in the house until she died. Then it would pass to Carol and me. But when Stephanie announced that she was going to sell the house and buy another with the proceeds, we found out that the very home we grew up in and were supposed to inherit we no longer had any claim to because Dad and Stephanie held it in joint tenancy.

Carol: I can't tell you how crushed I was. I just couldn't picture not going back to our childhood home or not being able to tend Mom's roses.

Joe: Poor Carol. Mom had always jokingly made her promise to take care of all her "other children" if anything happened to her, and she took it to heart. More important, though, this was to be a special place Carol and I would pass on to *our* children.

Carol: I just didn't understand what was going on? Why wouldn't we be entitled to inherit the house when Dad passed on, especially if it says so in his will? Isn't that enough?

Discussion

WHEN PROPERTY OR TITLE is held in joint tenancy, the unforeseen may occur, as we have seen with Carol and her brother Joe. Perhaps their dad didn't realize that they could be denied the intention of his will, once he was gone, by having placed his assets in joint tenancy with Stephanie. And, we can't be certain, but he may have put the property in joint tenancy thinking this protected Stephanie's right to remain there since he ultimately intended that his children would inherit it. As in so many situations I have seen regarding joint tenancy, things don't always turn out as planned.

Most people feel that they have taken the necessary steps to pass on their assets by simply putting those assets in joint tenancy with right of survivorship (WROS) or gifting them outright by signing over property while they are still alive. Joint tenancy WROS means that two or more people can hold title to a piece of property and the title of the property will transfer immediately into the name or names of the other or others when the death of one person occurs. Unlike a will, which must be probated, or proven, in a court, there are no court proceedings, no time delays, and no court fees with joint tenancy. In fact, as in the case of Joe and Carol, joint tenancy WROS will override the intent and instructions of a will. Holding property in joint tenancy could create a myriad of unexpected problems.

In addition to couples holding property in joint tenancy, many times an elderly parent may want to put your name on the title of his or her home or stock portfolio as joint tenant WROS. This usually happens because Dad or Mom feels more secure knowing that you will be able to take action should something happen to him or her. In a joint tenancy ownership you would have the legal right, in most situations, to manage the assets as needed. Also, once your last surviving parent dies, the process of inheriting the property requires only that you produce a death certificate, and the asset is then in your name. Or maybe you suggested this arrangement to Dad or Mom for the same reasons, and he or she agreed. Without knowing it, more problems may be created than avoided. The following are examples of what could happen.

Guidelines

THE IRS

The current law states that an individual can only give up to $10,000 per person per year. Whenever you give a gift of more than $10,000, you must file the appropriate paperwork, a gift-tax return, with the IRS. When your name is placed in joint tenancy, where you have not paid a reasonable price for your share of that property, you have essentially been given a gift. For example, if your name is put on your mom's house, valued at $350,000, you are receiving a gift of $175,000, or half the value of the house. Now your mom must file a "gift tax" return with the IRS (U.S. gift tax return/form 709). When doing so, she has two choices: She can pay the tax on any amount of more than $10,000 that she gives you, or she can request that the IRS deduct the amount of more than $10,000 from the 1998 maximum of $625,000 allowed to be inherited, estate-tax-free, upon her death. In our example, $165,000 must be reported one way or the other ($175,000, half the value of the house, minus $10,000, the allowable yearly gift, equals $165,000).

Most people neglect to file any paperwork at all. They think all they need to do is add the other individual's name to the property. But when a death occurs, a tax return must still be filed for the deceased. And there is a special section on the IRS forms that requires you to list all properties that the deceased held in joint tenancy. Once these are indicated, the IRS can question how those properties were acquired by you. Did you pay for them or were they gifted to you? If you say you paid for them, you must prove it. If they were gifted to you, the IRS will look for the requisite gift tax return to find out how much of the $625,000 was used up. If none was filed, the IRS has the right to assess penalties. This may sound like a rather remote occurrence, but your chances of getting caught will increase with the new advancements in technology.

You can see that holding property in joint tenancy, as simple a process as it may seem, can create extra paperwork as well as adding a large potential tax burden. But, there's more. . . .

CONSERVATORSHIP

As mentioned earlier, your name is usually placed on the property with Mom or Dad in case anything happens to that person. This enables you to sign documents and take care of business, if needed. But these good intentions of taking care of Mom or Dad could backfire.

Patricia and her mom, Nora, owned everything jointly—their home, investments, etc. Everything appeared to be going well until it was discovered that Nora had Alzheimer's disease. Eventually she needed to be placed in a nursing home, to be monitored carefully. When it was obvious that Nora wouldn't be returning to her home, Patricia needed to sell the house to help meet the expenses of her mom's ongoing care. At the close of escrow, Patricia was confronted with the fact that Nora had to sign the sales documents to sell the home. Nora, as joint tenant, was required to sign on all transactions. But her condition prevented her from comprehending and responding to a business transaction. This is where the trouble began. Patricia now had to go to court and have Nora declared incompetent and have the court appoint a conservator. Not only was this a lengthy and painful procedure, but also the court was now Patricia's new joint tenant. She needed the court's approval for any sale of property

TIP:

The amount that can be inherited estate-tax-free has a 1998 maximum of $625,000. If your name is on property valued at more than $625,000, whoever gave you the property will immediately be required to pay a gift tax on anything above this current $625,000 limit. If you do not pay this gift tax at the time it is due, penalties and assessments will be added to the total.

or investments she wanted to make as well as any use of the money. How could they have avoided these complications? Setting up a trust wherein Patricia was made trustee or successor trustee would have allowed her to act alone in legal matters without the interference of the courts.

LAWSUITS

When you hold property in joint tenancy WROS to protect your parents, any legal actions taken against you could directly affect the status of your parents' property. In the case of a lawsuit, if a judgment is levied against you, assets with your name on them as joint tenant could be seized or have a lien placed against them. If one of those assets that you hold in joint tenancy is the home your parents live in, they could be forced by the court to sell the property. Everyone's good intentions can turn into a situation severely jeopardizing your parents' financial security.

REVERSE MORTGAGES

Another obstacle with joint tenancy WROS is that reverse mortgages may no longer be obtainable. A reverse mortgage is one way in which an individual over sixty can get extra monthly income by using the equity that has accrued in the home (see page 181). Because the age of the applicant is pertinent, if your name is listed as joint tenant on your parents' property and you are not over sixty, it may not be possible for Mom or Dad to get that reverse mortgage.

Unexpected Problems

Usually people rely on the method of joint tenancy so they are assured their property will pass effortlessly to the person for whom it is intended. We have seen what some of the issues can be when passing property through joint tenancy, but there are other issues that must be addressed. Here are some more examples of what can happen. . . .

WHEN YOU WANT TO SELL YOUR HOME

Joint tenancy may put you in a position wherein you may not be able to sell your property.

When Bridget became a widow, she decided to put everything in joint tenancy with her daughter Hanna. Hanna was having serious marital problems with her husband, Colter, that ended in a separation. As Bridget's health changed, she decided to sell her home and move to a more likable climate. Just as the sale was to be finalized on her house, she was informed that she needed Colter's signature to sell because he was still legally married to her daughter Hanna, and was entitled to an interest in Hanna's half of Bridget's home. Bridget will not be able to do anything until Colter signs the papers (or until Hanna and Colter are finally divorced).

WHEN YOU HOLD TITLE WITH
YOUR MARRIED CHILD

Listen to Jill as she recounts the story of herself and her sisters:

> Our Mom, Lillian, had a wonderful house that she always planned to keep in the family. We four chil-

dren felt the same way about the house; someday it would make an ideal vacation home. After Dad died, she created a will that left everything to the four of us. It was Mom's next-door neighbor who told her that a will was okay to have, but if you really want to avoid probate for your children, you should put the name of one of the kids on the property title as a joint tenant. So Mom put our oldest sister, Beverly, who had recently married, on the property title as joint tenant. Since we four children were very close to one another, there was no question that when Mom died the house would belong to all of us.

Mom died and the house passed to Beverly as expected. Then the worst possible thing happened. Two weeks after Mom died, Beverly was killed in an automobile accident. Beverly's husband, whom none of us really got to know very well, claimed the house as the surviving spouse and was granted the house by the courts in accordance with Beverly's will. Beverly mentioned changing her will after Mom died but had never gotten around to it. While Beverly's husband vacations there, the three of us are still trying to get our mother's house back.

Even if Beverly had died without a will, in many states the laws would still have given Beverly's husband at least half the house and her siblings the other half. Regardless, it was a large price to pay simply to avoid the cost of setting up a trust.

WHEN YOU HOLD TITLE WITHOUT A WILL

It is not uncommon for husband and wife to hold their property in joint tenancy. In a first marriage, property tends to pass without difficulty. It is when there is a second marriage and property is intended for the children of one or the other that problems can arise.

Rick and Rona had both been divorced for several

years before they met and got married. Rona had two children from her previous marriage. Rick had none. Rona also brought property she had previously acquired into the new marriage. It was agreed by both that the property should rightfully be left to Rona's children after both Rick and Rona became deceased, so Rona made out a will stating so. Since Rick did not own anything, he did not bother to make out a will. A few years later, however, it was pointed out to them that Rick would not be protected if Rona died first, so they were advised that the easiest way to solve the problem was to put the property in joint tenancy. In this way the property could pass to Rick without going through probate.

Years later, Rona unexpectedly died of a heart attack, and, as they had been told, the property passed to Rick and was now solely in his name. Rick still had no will. When Rick died, his "estate" became what is referred to as *intestate*. Intestate means that an individual dies without a will, so the court must decide who receives the property. To do this, the court takes over management of the property and distributes it according to the succession laws of the state. Referred to as intestate succession, these laws are based on old English common law of lines of sanguinity. More commonly they are known as bloodlines.

The court determined that since Rick had no children and his parents were already deceased, all the property Rona and Rick had meant for her children would go to Rick's estranged brother. Rona's children, who were supposed to inherit the property, got nothing.

Holding property in joint tenancy with right of survivorship allows the property to pass efficiently, but it also means that the other person, or people, become the new owners of that property upon your death. No

TIP:

Be aware that holding property in joint tenancy with right of survivorship overrides the instructions of any will or trust. Make sure that a trust between spouses is written so that once one spouse dies, the other spouse may not alter or amend the provisions relating to the distribution of the deceased spouse's half of the marital property. Ask your attorney to explain the meaning of all amendments and provisions for changes in your trust.

matter what your will may have stated or your intentions may have been or what you believe will happen, the new owner or owners can do whatever they want with the property.

WHEN YOU HOLD TITLE WITH A WILL

Thelma and Nate had been married for forty-five years and had three children. They both wanted the kids to get everything they had worked so hard to acquire. So they both made wills clearly stating their wishes: Their property was to go to their children after they were both gone. Their assets were made up of one home and quite a large stock portfolio. Everything was held in joint tenancy, because that is generally how most married couples hold title.

Nate passed away first and, according to plan, everything transferred into Thelma's name. A few years later, Thelma remarried and, again, put everything into joint tenancy with her new husband, Ralph. She did this because she learned that this is how husband and wife hold property. She never felt she had cause to worry about her children receiving the property because her will left it all to them, not to Ralph.

When Thelma died, the home and the stock portfolio did *not* go to her children, as the will dictated. It went to her new husband because of how they held title. Even though the will stated that her children should receive the property and stocks, the joint tenancy with right of survivorship legally overrode the intent of Thelma's will. Ralph, of course, left everything to his children, not hers. Ouch!

JOINT TENANCY AND DIVORCE

Janine is a professor at one of the Big Ten universities. She fell in love with and married Mark, another professor there. They moved to Hawaii and bought their dream condo for $300,000, at the real estate market's high point. With 20 percent down, they financed $240,000. After only two years, Janine and Mark decided to divorce. They were unable to sell the condo because the market had taken a downturn and the condo was now worth only $200,000. Janine desperately wanted to get back to work on the mainland, so she left to settle into her new position as well as purchase a home on the mainland. It was agreed between the two of them before she left that Mark would keep the condo and make all the payments until he could refinance when the market recovered. Time passed, and before Mark could refinance, he died in an automobile accident. Now the financial responsibility for the condo, as well as ownership, reverted to Janine because her name was still on the mortgage and title. Worse yet, she discovered that Mark was in arrears with his payments. Since Janine had already purchased another home, she did not have the money to pay the back mortgage payments, and the bank foreclosed on the property. Not only did this ruin her credit rating, but her having been relieved of the mortgage debt placed her in jeopardy with the IRS. In the majority of the states*, the IRS considers the foreclosure on a personal residence to be a relief of debt and, as such, a taxable event. Janine is now liable for taxes on the "perceived debt"—the difference between the value of the property and what is owed on it. Since the value

---

*There are ten states where this ruling does not apply.

of the property is $200,000 and she still owes some $240,000, she will have to pay taxes on $40,000. Janine is now in serious trouble.

When you own property jointly, both names will most likely be on the mortgage. This may be okay while you are married, but make sure, should you divorce, that you are aware of the mortgage law in your particular state and that you address the potential liability risk of keeping your name on the title and loan in any divorce settlement so as to avoid a problem similar to Janine's.

JOINT TENANCY IN COMMUNITY PROPERTY STATES

Although joint tenancy is an efficient way for property to pass between spouses and avoid probate, if you live in a community property state* and you intend to sell property after your spouse has died, you will lose an income tax advantage by holding property in joint tenancy as opposed to in community property. Here's why:

WHEN TITLE IS HELD IN JOINT TENANCY ON PROPERTY OTHER THAN REAL ESTATE

Let's say you and your spouse bought stock many years ago for $30,000 and held it in joint tenancy. That $30,000 is considered the cost-basis of the stock for income tax purposes, which means that when you sell the stock, you will owe capital gains tax on any amount you receive over $30,000. Because you own the stock in joint tenancy with your spouse, the cost

---

*The community property states are: Arizona, California, Louisiana, Nevada, New Mexico, Texas, and Washington.

basis is evenly split between the two of you: $15,000 to you and $15,000 to your spouse.

When your spouse dies, because you held the stock in joint tenancy, you are entitled to receive an increase in the original cost basis of your deceased spouse's half. This is known as a "step-up in cost basis." If the stock is valued at $350,000 at the time your spouse dies, his or her half is now increased or stepped up to $175,000. Your cost basis of $15,000 remains the same. Now that you own the stock by yourself, your new cost basis on the stock is $190,000 ($15,000 plus $175,000). If you sell the stock for $350,000, you will only owe taxes on $160,000 ($350,000 − $190,000 = $160,000), or about $32,000 at the maximum 20% tax rate.

This step-up in cost basis saves you money in taxes when you sell the stock, but the savings are even greater if you are in a community property state and you hold title in community property rather than joint tenancy.

TITLE HELD IN COMMUNITY PROPERTY

As in joint tenancy, each spouse will have an original cost basis of $15,000 on the $30,000 stock. However, when your spouse dies, not only do you receive a step-up in cost basis on his or her half, but you receive it on your half as well.

In our example, if the stock is valued at $350,000 when your spouse dies, you get a step-up in cost basis on the stock to $350,000. Now if you sell the stock for $350,000, you will owe absolutely nothing in capital gains taxes. By holding the stock in community property rather than joint tenancy, you would have saved $32,000 in taxes.

The Outright Gifting of Property

Instead of putting property in joint tenancy, parents will sometimes "gift outright," or transfer the property title or stock portfolios or bank accounts, etc., into their son's or daughter's name. Outright gifting is generally done after one of the parents has died and for the following reasons:

- for estate tax planning purposes (in large estates);
- to avoid probate (Mom or Dad feels they are somehow saving their children the trouble and expense of going through probate when it comes time to inherit the property);
- to avoid the cost of setting up a trust (Mom or Dad would rather give the property now than pay $1,000 to $2,000 in fees);
- to protect assets against depletion in case of a long-term-care illness (by gifting assets to the children, Mom or Dad may then qualify for government assistance—Medicaid—to help pay for the cost of a nursing home).

While there are some cases where outright gifting has merit, it also can backfire. Therefore it is important to understand and to be able to avoid the pitfalls of gifting.

EXPECT THE UNEXPECTED

No one expects parents to outlive their children, but this is a potential danger of outright gifting. If the plan is to take care of Mom or Dad and you have received assets from them for safekeeping, should you predecease them, what will happen to their future? Depending on how your estate is set up, it is possible that your parents may end up in probate court just to get their assets back, costing them thousands of dollars. It is also possible that they could lose their property altogether if you have not included your parents as beneficiary to that part of your estate. A will that designates Mom or Dad as beneficiary is not sufficient because it would require those assets to be probated, taking a significant amount of time and, most likely, money.

Ina was still spry at eighty but knew her limitations. Her main concern at her age was that something might happen to her requiring nursing home care. To qualify for Medicaid assistance in case it was necessary, she gifted her assets, valued at $400,000, to her son, George. Several years passed and everything was fine when, suddenly, George died of a massive coronary. He had no wife or children, no sisters or brothers, so he bequeathed all of his belongings back to his mother first via his will. Ina got everything back, all right, but it took months, and during that time she didn't have access to any of her funds because they were bogged down in the probate procedure. The worst part was that it cost Ina about $20,000 in fees to get her own property back. She also used $390,000 of her $625,000 unified credit.

Any assets you already have been gifted, or expect to receive for safekeeping, require that you take the necessary precautions to protect Mom or Dad in case something happens to you. The best way to protect them, and to bypass probate, would be to put those assets in a living revocable trust. As a provision of the trust you will need to designate what happens to Mom or Dad's property. Does it stay in trust and another relative takes over as trustee? Or does it revert to Mom or Dad?

GIFTING TO AVOID PROBATE

Because people know that probate is a lengthy and expensive procedure, they will gift their assets, while alive, knowing this will avoid the hassle of probate later on.

As with joint tenancy, gifting can become an expensive proposition. Using the same asset as in our joint tenancy example, you have been gifted your parents' stock, originally purchased for $30,000. This $30,000 is considered the cost basis of the stock. Because you are given the stock while Mom or Dad is still alive, this becomes your cost basis as well. However, when you sell that stock, you will own taxes on the difference between your cost basis ($30,000) and the selling price for the stock. If the sale price is $350,000, you will owe taxes on $320,000 ($350,000 minus the cost basis of $30,000).

Remember, when you inherit property, you get that step-up in cost basis to the market value of the stock at the time you inherit it. If it is valued at $350,000 and you sell it for $350,000, there is no gain, thus no tax. If you had inherited the stock through a trust, you would have no probate fees or income taxes upon selling it. It is true that if you gift property, you will avoid probate, but it may be at the expense of paying an enormous amount in income taxes.

GIFTING TO QUALIFY FOR MEDICAID*

If gifting is being considered to ensure qualifying for Medicaid, here's what you need to know: In most states, one's home is considered an exempt asset when qualifying for Medicaid. As long as it is stated that Mom or Dad intends to return to live there after a long-term-care stay, regardless of the value of the home, it will not be considered when determining Medicaid eligibility.† So if all Mom or Dad owns is his or her house and nothing more, that person could still qualify for assistance.

It is the assets—cash, stocks, bonds, etc.—that cannot exceed a certain amount for someone to qualify for Medicaid. To be Medicaid eligible in most states, you cannot have more than $2,000 in assets, so determining which assets to gift is significant. It is also important to realize that gifting any asset other than "cash" money may have tax ramifications. The laws regarding Medicaid eligibility vary from state to state and are continually changing and becoming more restrictive. It is extremely important that you contact an elder-law attorney or estate planner before you gift assets simply to qualify for Medicaid assistance. Gifting or transferring assets is not as easy as it seems.

On August 5, 1997, President Clinton signed into law Section 4734 of the Balanced Budget Bill (HR2015), amending the Health Insurance Portability and Accountability Act of 1996. Under the amended law, any service provider who advises a senior client to dispose of income in order to receive Medicaid benefits will be fined, imprisoned, or both. Seniors, although no longer subject to fines or imprisonment,

> **TIP:**
>
> †The length of time a home can be held by the owner while in a long-term-care stay varies from state to state. In some cases a house is protected for as little as six months before it must be sold to pay for continued care.

---

*In the state of California this is known as MediCal.

will continue to face ineligibility periods for such improper transfers.

One last thought before gifting any assets to qualify for Medicaid: Look into long-term-care insurance as an alternative (see page 79). If it is affordable for you or your parent or parents at the time, it should be seriously considered. Medicaid is not a panacea for taking care of your long-term-care needs. Medicaid, by definition, is welfare. The available nursing homes accepting Medicaid patients is limited, and waiting lists for openings may make this option unsuitable. On the other hand, a holder of a long-term-care policy is considered a private-pay patient, and the selection of nursing home facilities is far more extensive than with Medicaid.

THOSE OTHER NIFTY GIFTING PROBLEMS

Anytime a gift is made of anything worth over $10,000, the donor must file the correct gift tax return with the IRS. And, just as in joint tenancy, if you are involved in a lawsuit and assets are confiscated as part of the judgment, they'll take what Mom or Dad gave you, and Mom or Dad could end up "high and dry." If Mom or Dad ever needs the extra income she or he could get from a reverse mortgage, unless *you* are over sixty, property you hold for them will not qualify.

There are valid reasons for gifting, but never take it upon yourself to make this decision without seeking professional advice and guidance in these areas:

- What is the purpose of gifting?
- Does it make sense in your particular situation?
- If gifting is warranted, what assets should be gifted?

- What plans have been set in place by the recipient in case something unexpected happens?
- Is there another way to achieve your goal?

Currently, one way to avoid the problems you may encounter with joint tenancy and gifting may be to set up a trust. Trusts are not as complicated as once thought. Trusts are not just for the wealthy. Trusts do not have to cost you a fortune to set up. There is no mystery when inheriting via a trust. *If you really want to give your family a gift, give them a trust!*

chapter 4

Durable Power of Attorney for Health Care

John's heart surgery was Monday morning. He finally decided to sign a durable power of attorney for health care right after our Father's Day barbecue on Sunday. By then it was too late!

Barbara's Story

To give you some background, John had been ill with coronary heart disease for fourteen years before his death. He had had his first bypass surgery eleven years earlier. Because of severe arterial degeneration, he needed a second surgery. But something inside John told him not to expect to survive this one. He even commented that he didn't want to be on a respirator or life-saving machines if anything went wrong with the surgery. We finally agreed, as a precaution, to have John sign the durable power of attorney for health care papers we had tucked away in the drawer. We would do this before the weekend was over because his surgery was Monday morning.

On Saturday I went to the supermarket to shop for our annual Father's Day family barbecue. When I returned several hours later, I saw John slumped over in his chair with the TV still on. My God, I knew he was dead, but I didn't know what else to do, so I called 911. He wasn't breathing and was even purple from lack of oxygen when the paramedics arrived. They worked to resuscitate him because his body was still somewhat warm. After half an hour of this, his heart started. While John was being transported by ambulance, they lost and revived him another time. So when we got to the hospital, I found the doctors and asked that John not be put on life support. But I was too late. By the time we arrived, they had already hooked him up. I was powerless to take him off the machines because we didn't have the durable power of attorney for health care.

There was a three-day waiting period before they would test for brain activity. John showed none, only minimal brain stem activity that helped pump his heart, but that was all. With the aid of our attorney, Janet, the neurologist at the hospital agreed that the situation was hopeless. Fortunately, the doctor didn't believe in unnecessarily keeping people alive mechanically.

Now the worst part was about to begin. Taking someone off life support is far more difficult than putting that person on. The machines aren't turned off all at once; it's done little by little, one machine at a time, over an eight-hour period. You just have to sit there and watch this person you love leave you slowly.

Discussion

UNDER ANY CIRCUMSTANCES, it is extremely difficult to lose someone you love, but it is inevitable. It will happen to all of us.

To give you further background, Barbara was my secretary at the time this happened to John. Knowing their situation, I discussed a trust and a *durable power of attorney for health care* (DPAHC) with them. They set up the trust with my associate, Janet, who specializes in trusts and wills, but they took the DPAHC papers home to think things through. From time to time I asked her if they had signed the DPAHC papers. When she indicated they had not gotten around to it, I reminded her of its importance. When John was on life support at the hospital, the doctors did not simply take him off because Barbara asked them to; he continued to show signs of minimal brain stem activity. It was Janet who was fully aware of their intentions and went to bat for them, taking responsibility for the final decision. Ordinarily this would not have happened. Janet knew that John had been ill for many years, in and out of the hospital, and the lifetime maximum on his health insurance was close to being reached. Under these circumstances it wouldn't have been long before his insurance reached its maximum lifetime coverage and Barbara would be responsible for the bills. We knew the loss of John would be hard enough; we didn't want Barbara to be financially ruined as well. This is one factor you should check on your health insurance policy—the maximum lifetime coverage.

What is a durable power of attorney for health care? Simply, it is a document created while you are still capable of expressing your desires regarding medical treatment and life support. It gives someone you designate the authority to take you off life support if there is no hope you will ever live without the machines, or to make other health care decisions if you are unable to make them yourself. If you do not have this written authority, it would be virtually impossible to take your loved one off any life support system, even if you knew this is what that person would have wanted. Haven't we all given some thought to this situation? But how many of us have acted on it?

If John had been conscious he would have had the right to decide if he wanted to terminate any medical treatment, including life support systems, himself. But he was not. There was no way for anyone at the hospital to know what his desires were without a written document with those wishes clearly stated. Several well-publicized judicial decisions state that life support cannot be cut off while patients are comatose or unconscious and therefore unable to state their desires.

This does not have to happen to anyone. With a DPAHC or similar document, you can be assured that if you become incapacitated, your desires about being hooked up to life support systems will be respected. The DPAHC is well accepted by the medical profession and is legally valid in all fifty states.

The now famous U.S. Supreme Court case *Curzon* v. *Missouri* tested the "right to die" issue. The young woman involved, who had been in an automobile accident, was placed on feeding tubes because her feelings about not being placed on life support were not expressed in writing. Two important determinations came out of this case: *There is such a thing as a right to die; and you cannot exercise this right unless you put your wishes in writing.* Once you have decided in favor of a durable power of attorney for health care, the more difficult decision is who will make all the important decisions for you when the time comes.

Guidelines

DECISIONS TO MAKE

When completing a DPAHC, to eliminate any confusion regarding your wishes concerning life support, the Trauma Foundation in San Francisco has drawn up the following guidelines. You will be allowed to choose only one.

1. I want my life to be prolonged as long as possible, without regard to my condition, my chances for recovery, or the cost of the procedures.
2. I want life-sustaining treatment to be pro-

vided unless I am in a coma or persistent vegetative state, which two doctors, including my attending physician, reasonably conclude in writing to be irreversible. If my doctors have reached this conclusion, I do not want life-sustaining treatment to be provided or continued.

3. I do *not* want my life to be artificially or forceably prolonged, unless there is some hope that both my physical and mental health may be restored, and I do not want life-sustaining treatment to be provided or continued if the burdens of the treatment outweigh the expected benefits. I want my agent to consider the relief of suffering and the quality of the possible extension of my life in making decisions concerning life-sustaining treatment. At all times my dignity shall be maintained.

It is when you become incapacitated and cannot make any decisions, that you leave the responsibility to someone else to determine the "what if" scenarios. This person, or your agent, is legally known as your attorney-in-fact. The responsibility is tremendous so *that person should be someone whose judgment you trust.*

YOUR AGENT

No matter how specific you try to be in the DPAHC, since no one can foresee the actual circumstances under which it is to be used, a fair amount of discretion will have to be exercised by this person. You will want someone who is most philosophically aligned with your position. Ask yourself: Who knows you best and will know and agree with what you want? Will that person be able to act intelligently and according to your wishes when the circumstances arises? Be sure you discuss your wishes with your agent well in advance of any life-threatening situation.

The person you choose to be your agent should love you and care about you but be strong enough to do the right thing and not give in to others who may be more emotionally attached not to letting you go. If you have a particular religious or spiritual bent, your belief should be reflected in your choice of an agent. It is better to have someone as your agent who lives no more than a day's travel away.

HOW DOES THE PERSON FEEL ABOUT ACTING AS YOUR AGENT?

After you have thought about who you would like to be your agent, ask that person how he or she feels about it. Is there any hesitation on that person's part? If so, find out what it is. This may not be the right person. Remember, it is not an easy job. Make all your wishes known and make sure the individual you have chosen feels comfortable in carrying them out. I have selected someone whom I know will be strong enough to carry out my wishes, but not necessarily the person who is closest to me.

COAGENTS

Many of you may have more than one child and feel you want to make all the children coagents. You can do this, but it is still unclear about what happens if there is disagreement between or among the coagents. So, most likely, no action will be taken if they disagree, making the DPAHC worthless. For most people it is best to designate one person as the primary agent or attorney-in-fact. Generally, in a situation where there is more than one child, it is very rare that one will not consult the other or others.

HAVING A BACKUP AGENT

Always name alternate agents in your DPAHC. At least three people should be named. If something happens to the first person named, you then have a second choice and even a third choice.

GLITCHES

In a family situation not everyone may agree with your wishes. Even if one child agrees with you and is your agent, another child may defy the order even though he or she may not be your agent. That person can go to court to try to stop the proceedings, alleging that you did not know what you were doing when you signed the papers.

If, after talking to all your family members, you sense there may be a difficult situation, make sure your durable power of attorney for health care states: "I want the wishes of my agent to be respected regardless of the contrary wishes or intentions of other members of my family."

BE CLEAR WITH WHAT YOU WANT

After you have chosen the person or people who will be acting as your agent and they have agreed to it, then it is important to make their job as easy as possible. The more explicit your written instructions, the less possible confusion or guilt will result.

Generally we all want to live as long as possible, so you will need to be clear under which circumstances you would no longer want to be kept alive. You must ask yourself some very pointed questions. What are your personal feelings about the practice of prolonging life with machines? How far is too far? Have you ever seen someone on life support? Some courts have made the distinction between being hooked up to a machine that pumps your heart and lungs and being kept alive by intravenous or feeding tubes. Do you consider these the same, or are you more inclined to agree with having a respiratory device detached but continue being fed intravenously or via a tube? To help you make determinations, consider visiting someone on life support to see that person's quality of life, and discuss it with the doctor.

CHECK WITH YOUR DOCTOR AND HOSPITAL

Know how your doctor and the hospital he or she affiliates with feel about your wishes. If your doctor or the hospital does not agree with your wishes, it might be wise to seek a new physician or hospital.

PUTTING THOSE DECISIONS TO WORK

Now that you know who will make the decision and what that person or those persons are to do, you need to make sure that your wishes are accurately written in the proper format.

THE DOCUMENT

Most states have enacted legislation that prescribes the format of the durable power of attorney for health care form. Forms can be procured at most hospitals or public health services in your area. They may even have someone on staff to help you fill out the form.

I send my clients to an attorney who is up to date in this matter, can provide them with the standardized form for their state, and can assist them in filling it out. Also, if there is a special situation, a particular illness involved, or if you need a more detailed description of life support systems, an attorney can make sure it is covered by personalizing the form.

WHEN TO FILL OUT THE PAPERWORK

Take care of this task sooner rather than later. Barbara and John had been handed the paperwork to sign but put it off. Tragedies can occur to people of all ages, so everyone should have a durable power of attorney for health care. It is unfortunate that the most dramatic cases concern young people. The law requires, however, that you be an adult to express your wishes in a DPAHC.

Remember, unless you have this *in writing*, the doctors do not have to abide by your wishes. This has become an issue because of the many lawsuits in the recent past. There is a case where a couple had been in a car wreck. Both were injured, but the husband had been put on life support. When the wife recovered and understood from the doctor that her husband would never recover and would remain in a vegetative state, she requested that he be unhooked. He was. There was a nurse present who opposed the actions of the doctor. She went so far as to send protesters to the doctor's house and to bring manslaughter charges against him. The charges were ultimately dropped. For reasons like this, unless there is a durable power of attorney for health care in writing, doctors and hospitals will no longer take a chance. They will protect themselves even at emotional and financial cost to you.

THE COST OF A DPAHC

A durable power of attorney for health care should cost no more than $75 to $150 when done through an attorney.

WHERE TO KEEP THE DOCUMENT

The completed form should be kept with whomever you have chosen to act as your agent. Additional copies should be made for your personal physician, HMO, or health insurance company and be kept as part of your medical records file. This will be helpful in circumstances where you are away from home. When your insurance plan or physician is contacted in case of injury, they will let it will be known, too, that you have a DPAHC. For security purposes, always carry the name of your doctor, HMO, or insurance company in your wallet or purse.

UPDATING YOUR DPAHC

If you have appointed a parent as your agent and that parent dies, or if a particular relationship changes, like divorce or remarriage, you will need to update your DPAHC.

A POWER OF ATTORNEY AND A DURABLE POWER OF ATTORNEY ARE NOT THE SAME

A power of attorney simply has to do with assets management and the ability to change and take control of those assets. *The durable power of attorney for health care deals only with health care issues.*

TIP:

If you are going to set up a trust with an attorney, the DPAHC should be included in the overall price of the work.

A LIVING WILL AND A DURABLE POWER OF ATTORNEY FOR HEALTH CARE ARE NOT THE SAME

A living will expresses your general wishes about critical care. It does not authorize anyone to act on your behalf to make decisions. A living will is interpreted by the doctors as a directive. A directive, or advance directive, does not give them the power to unplug you. In many states you must first be diagnosed with a terminal illness and then have signed the living will for it to be valid. Living wills are filled out on approved forms, and they cannot be changed in any significant way to meet your further wishes. A living will does not handle this matter as efficiently and effectively as a durable power of attorney for health care.

The durable power of attorney for health care is the most important document you will have—more than a will or a trust—because it affects you directly. A will and a trust deal only with money matters after you are gone. This document deals with your life. In the past it was a private matter between the doctors and the family. Usually you could count on your doctor to do what was necessary. But because this is such a new area of law, because we are in an age of litigation, polarization, and divergent philosophical and religious beliefs, you cannot count on the doctor anymore.

When I asked Barbara why John hadn't signed the durable power of attorney for health care over the eleven years he knew he was seriously ill, she said, "He just couldn't bring himself to face his own death, and signing a paper like this makes it a reality. This may be one of the hardest things you will ever have to do, but that still shouldn't stop you."

Long-Term-Care Insurance: Buy Now or Pay (a Lot More) Later

Nothing is more preventable than the swift and total financial devastation that comes from a long-term-care stay. That is why I consider this the most important chapter in this book.

Suze's Story

Early in my career as a financial advisor, I decided to specialize in retirement planning, to make sure that when my clients were no longer able or wanted to work, they would have the funds needed to sustain them throughout their old age. I also wanted to make sure that if they became ill they had enough money so they would never have to go to a nursing home. I was quite adamant that no client of mine would ever end up that way. I guess I felt this way because my aunt worked in a nursing home in Chicago, where I would often accompany her to visit with the residents. I loved to talk to the people as much as they enjoyed my visits. Most fixed in my memory, though, was the sadness I detected in their eyes. My youth and inexperience led me to believe it was simply because they had no money that they lived in the nursing home rather than their own homes. Interestingly, both my grandparents ended up in this very same nursing home. I naively thought they were there under the same circumstances. In my role as a financial advisor, I discovered that people didn't end up in nursing homes because they had no money; they had no money because they ended up in nursing homes.

It wasn't until I met my clients Bernice and Conrad that I saw, firsthand, how a long-term-care stay could ruin the lives in a family.

When this pleasant, soft-spoken couple came to me, I thought they had the perfect financial situation for retirement. Their monthly expenses were $3,000. Their income came from their pension of $2,000 a month, and they received $1,000 a month from their retirement account, which had $160,000 in it and which I invested partly for growth and partly for this income. Bernice and Conrad were several years away from receiving Social Security, so I set up a mortgage payment program for them to complete their house payments by the time their Social Security payments started. This, along with the money invested for growth, would be their hedge against inflation and illness. With the house paid off, their expenses would go down. Their income would then increase even more, when Social Security began. I thought that if anything happened to them, their extra income would take care of it. This was an ideal plan—or so I thought. Everything went according to schedule until a year and a half after Conrad retired. He had a stroke. Bernice tried her best to keep Conrad at home, but she just could not care for him physically when the in-home help she hired wasn't reliable. Six months later he ended up in a nursing home at a cost of $3,000 a month. All their current income, all $3,000 of it, went to Conrad's care. What was Bernice to do? She still had the $3,000 monthly expenses at home to deal with. The only way for her to survive was to start taking principal from the invested retirement money.

Bernice was required to withdraw nearly $40,000 from the IRA principal to secure the full $36,000 in annual income she needed. The $4,000 excess paid the taxes, since these were pretax funds she was withdrawing. Now they only had $120,000 left in their account, generating $750 a month in earnings ($9,000 annually compared to the $12,000 they received before). This left them $3,000 short to pay for Conrad's nursing home. The following year they were required to take out even more money to make up the difference, leaving them, once again, short on interest income. Within three years the IRA was wiped out.

Shortly afterward, Conrad died. Bernice still receives the $2,000-a-month pension (Conrad was smart enough to take the 100 percent joint and survivor benefit—see Chapter Seven) but still falls short $1,000 each month to meet her own expenses.

Discussion

THE STORY of Bernice and Conrad was a hard lesson to learn. The fact that one out of three people will end up in a nursing home after age sixty-five only confirms the need to protect our assets. Today, when I ask my clients if they think a long-term-care stay could happen to them, almost unanimously the answer is *no*. Most even went so far as to say that if it did happen, they wouldn't worry because their health insurance or Medicare would pay for it. Health insurance and Medicare were not set up to cover these costs. Basically it is you, the consumer, who will bear the burden of payments unless you become financially destitute and Medicaid takes over payments.

If you do get to that point (and the chances are good, since 45 percent of all people in nursing homes are on Medicaid), the government can come back to your estate, demand restitution for your care, and collect by placing a lien on your property. What should your course of action be? The best and most affordable protection for your retirement may be long-term-care insurance.

When I first learned about long-term-care (LTC) insurance back in 1988, the policies were shortsighted, not worth the paper they were written on. In just about every case, the only ones who benefited from a LTC policy were the insurance companies who issued them. Today that is no longer true. LTC insurance provides the protection needed for older Americans. It is one of the most important parts of any retirement plan. Important enough, in fact, that many states are starting a co-venture arrangement with specific insurance companies, called a "public/private partnership" to make long-term-care insurance accessible to the public. Even though the state initiative for long-term care is open to all states, at the writing of this book only four states are offering this plan: California, Indiana, Connecticut, and New York. Some of you may be in a position to decide between the two alternatives: a private policy you buy on your own or one that is part of the state partnership arrangement. It is important to decide which policy provides the more cost effective way to purchase LTC insurance. Our in-depth discussion of LTC insurance will give you the ammunition to compare a private policy with a partnership policy (if it is available in your state) or to help decide which private policy is best for you so you can get the most for your money.

Before proceeding to the guidelines and an in-depth discussion of LTC insurance, here are some preliminary definitions and explanations.

WHAT IS LONG-TERM CARE?

Long-term care is any type of support and care you may need over an extended time. It includes help with such things as bathing and dressing, shopping, preparing meals, transportation, housecleaning, or a facility stay.

WHAT ARE THE CHANCES YOU WILL NEED LONG-TERM CARE?

After the age of sixty-five, most people have a fifty-fifty chance of needing some type of long-term care. Though more than half of those individuals needing to spend time in a nursing home will have to stay fewer than ninety days, the rest will stay an average of 2.9 years. Women in particular are more prone to be destined for long-term-care services. They live longer than men and, as a result, tend to develop more chronic ailments requiring health care and social services.

THE COST OF LONG-TERM-CARE SERVICES

Depending on the amount of care provided and your locale, the cost of care in nursing homes averages $30,000 to $100,000 a year and is increasing. In-home service costs can vary even more greatly, depending on what is needed, how long it is needed, and who provides the service. Estimates range from $8,500 to $70,000 a year. Unfortunately, most of you will pay for this care from your savings—the money you have worked for and saved during your lifetime—because *existing health insurance plans do not cover long-term care.* Major medical plans—Medicare, Medigap policies, and other pension health plans—either don't cover long-term-care needs or provide very restrictive and limited benefits. Even the newest national health care reform does not adequately address this issue. In the "baby boomer to be senior" decade of the 1990s, 25 percent of the annual Medicaid budget supports the 2 percent to 3 percent of Medicaid patients in nursing homes, the cost is so great. Common sense tells us that the government cannot possibly pay for long-term care when this age group becomes our largest-ever throng of seniors. So the government is trying to shift us toward Long Term Care insurance. Beginning in January 1997, if you purchase an LTC insurance policy that meets certain definitions established by The Health Insurance Portability and Accountability Act of 1996, or if you already had purchased an LTC policy prior to January 1, 1997, your premiums within limits may be itemized as tax deductions for medical expenses. Medical expense deductions are currently limited to the excess over 7.5 percent of a taxpayers adjusted gross income. [For more information about policy qualification, call Health Insurance Counseling and Advocacy Program (HICAP) at 800-434-0222 to find your local HICAP office.] Slowly but surely, it will pay in more ways than one to have an LTC insurance policy. Until things change dramatically, most people will turn to the two government-run health insurance programs to cover long-term-care services: Medicare and Medicaid (MediCal in California). Here is how these programs work:

THE MYTH OF MEDICARE

Most people believe that Medicare will pay for all their long-term-care expenses. It does not. Fewer than 2 percent of the long-term-care costs in our nation is covered by Medicare. The coverage is restrictive and pays for such care only if you meet very strict criteria:

- *You must be in an acute-care hospital for three days before entering the "skilled" nursing facility.* An acute-care hospital is an institution licensed by the state and legally qualified to provide skilled care.
- *The "skilled" nursing facility must be Medicare-certified.* Skilled care is medical care that can only be performed by or under the supervision of licensed nursing personnel.
- *Your care must be defined by Medicare as "skilled" care, not custodial care.* Custodial care is what most people receive by attendants in nursing facilities. It is not defined as medical care, as is skilled care.

When Medicare does pay for your skilled nursing care, it pays the full amount for the first twenty days only. For the next eighty days you must pay $81.50 a day before Medicare will pay the rest. After the one hundred days are up, you must pay the entire amount.

With in-home health care, the same limitations apply. Medicare covers only a small portion of home health care and only if it meets the criteria of skilled nursing care.

THE REALITY OF MEDICAID

Medicaid (called MediCal in California) is a combined federal and state program that covers medical care for the poor of all ages. To qualify for Medicaid (a form of welfare) means that you have become financially destitute. *If you do not plan for the expense of long-term care, it is likely that you will end up on Medicaid.*

In studies of individuals entering a nursing home, it has been shown that half of those on Medicaid were not indigent when they originally entered the facility. They had to "spend down" their assets until nothing was left before Medicaid took over. For married couples, the key issue is that qualifying for Medicaid can be devastating for the spouse still at home. He or she is left with little to survive on while trying to ensure that the ill spouse receives the care needed.

On Medicaid, your choice of skilled nursing facilities can be limited. And with the increasing number of older people needing long-term care, there may be long waiting lists for patients whose care will be covered by Medicaid. The financial strain placed on our Medicaid system has prompted the government to take steps to ensure that Medicaid is available to those who are truly financially destitute. As amended by Section 4734 of the Balanced Budged Bill (HR2015), Section 217 of the Health Insurance Portability and Accountability Act of 1996 makes it a criminal offense to dispose of assets in order to obtain Medicaid benefits primarily to pay for nursing home care. Advisors risk jail time and/or fines, and seniors face ineligibility periods for improper transfers. This law sends a clear message to the American public: private insurance should be purchased to pay for long-term care.

YOUR FAMILY AS SUPPORT

One final avenue available for help with long-term care needs is your family. It has been well documented that families provide some 70 percent to 80 percent of all home health and long-term care for older family members. Few families today are prepared financially, emotionally, and psychologically to maintain this intensive level of support for an extended time. Everyone in the family is impacted, with the major burden resting on women, who may be raising children and working at the same time parents need to be cared for.

Besides the emotional drain, families can exhaust their financial resources when caring for a family member. There may be a way to avoid becoming a financial burden on your family by planning for your long-term-care needs through the purchase of long-term-care insurance.

The guidelines, along with advice from a professional, will explain the workings of long-term-care insurance, how to purchase a policy, and the cost of a policy, and will provide you with a buyer's checklist. This list should alert you to some basic considerations when deciding which company, plan, and coverage options will meet your particular needs.

Guidelines

LONG-TERM-CARE INSURANCE

LTC insurance is specifically written to help cover the costs of long-term-care services within a skilled nursing facility, other settings, and a variety of home health care situations. The purpose of purchasing LTC insurance is to protect your assets.

Premiums, or the annual cost of insurance, will be based on your age at the time of purchase. The younger you are, of course, the lower the cost of the insurance. Everyone age forty-nine or older is a candidate for an LTC insurance policy. *Regardless of your age at the time of purchase, the total cost for the LTC policy will be less than the cost of one year in a nursing home* (see Table A on page 95 and Table B on page 97).

When I discuss long-term-care insurance with clients, they ask why they should pay for something they may never use. But isn't this exactly what you are doing when you buy auto or fire insurance, protecting yourself against the eventuality?

Consider these insurance statistics:

- One of 1,200 will use their fire insurance.
- One of 240 will use their automobile insurance.
- *One of three will use their long-term-care insurance policy.*

Certainly, long-term-care insurance is not for everyone. If you are not able to pay your bills, or if it takes every penny to make ends meet, you should not be purchasing an LTC policy. LTC insurance should be a consideration if your assets, excluding your home and car, are more than $50,000; if your annual income is more than $25,000; and if you are able to save some of your income after all your expenses have been met.

Do not make the mistake of thinking you can wait until you are sixty-five or seventy to take out this insurance. The cost, if you wait, could be too prohibitive. It is by *planning now* that you can secure your future at lower cost.

THE LONG-TERM-CARE PLAN: WHAT TO EXPECT AND WHAT TO LOOK FOR

DAILY BENEFIT

The amount of money your plan will pay for eligible care is the daily benefit. Policies generally offer $50 to $240 a day for nursing care and $40 to $150 a day for home health care.

Guideline: The average nursing care cost is $100 a day or $35,000 annually. If you want to buy a plan that will cover 100 percent of your costs, consider buying a daily benefit of $80 to $100.

BENEFIT PERIOD

This is the length of time your plan will pay benefits. Available benefit periods range from two years to a lifetime.

Guideline: The average nursing care stay is 2.9 years. If you are between ages forty-five and sixty-four, consider selecting a four-year to lifetime benefit. If you are older than sixty-four, choosing a four- to six-year option is adequate. The final choice, however, will depend on how much you can afford to pay in premiums. Premiums will be higher for a longer benefit period.

INFLATION OPTION

When purchasing a plan, you do so with the idea that you may need it sometime in the future. For this reason, always check policies for the inflation option provision. With this provision, your daily benefit increases a certain percentage each year to help keep pace with rising long-term-care costs. Often the inflation factor that is used is an annual increase of 5 percent simple interest or 5 percent compounded interest. Some policies will cap this growth by the amount or by an age limitation. Other policies will allow you to increase your daily benefit amount every three to four years by purchasing additional insurance at your current age rate. This will be one of the most important decisions you will make regarding an LTC insurance plan. The younger you are when you purchase the plan, the more time there is for the daily benefit to grow (see Table D for inflation on page 99).

Guideline:

• If you are between ages forty and sixty-five, the more beneficial choice will be the 5 percent compounded benefit with no age limit or financial cap, if you can afford it.

• From sixty-five to seventy, if money is an issue, consider the 5 percent simple interest choice. If cost is not an issue, the 5 percent compounded benefit is always the preferred choice.

• After age seventy, the decision to buy an inflation option will depend on your particular situation. In some cases it may be more economical to buy a larger daily benefit amount—say, $150 a day versus $100 a day, with no inflation increase—to accomplish the same goal.

ELIMINATION PERIOD

Similar to a deductible in your major medical health insurance plan, this is the time period during initial confinement for which you receive no paid benefits. These periods typically run from zero to ninety days. During this time you are responsible for covering all costs.

Guideline: Compare the premium costs between a shorter elimination period (zero to thirty days) and a longer period (sixty to ninety days). You may find that the difference in premium costs is not significant. In this case, *always consider buying the shortest possible elimination period you can afford to protect your assets and estate adequately. If a zero-day elimination period is offered and the price difference is insignificant, don't hesitate: Take it!*

NONFORFEITURE BENEFIT

Many companies offer a rider to their plans that indicates that if you do not use the benefits of your plan after a certain number of years, you or your beneficiaries can get back a portion of the money paid in premiums.

Guideline: Do not be fooled into believing this is easy money. It looks attractive, but be aware that the premium cost is usually about 35 percent higher for this rider. If you can afford the extra 35 percent and are disciplined, take that amount and invest it for growth. Ultimately you will come out ahead.

HOME HEALTH CARE (HHC)

This benefit covers the type of care you receive in your own home by a "home health care agency" licensed therapist and/or a homemaker or chore worker. The trend is to provide more care at home. And since most prefer being cared for in their own home, coverage for home health care is advantageous.

The costs will vary depending on the type of care needed, who provides the care, and for how long. Most LTC plans offering home health care protection provide a daily benefit of 50 percent to 80 percent of your skilled nursing care coverage.

Guideline: A home health care benefit that covers at least two years or 730 visits is recommended. Whether to consider more or less coverage will depend on other aspects of your plan. Some states require purchase of a minimum home health care benefit. This minimum is tied to the length of the benefit you choose for long-term-care coverage. Be sure to check this proviso in your state.

ALTERNATIVE PLAN FOR CARE

Many companies allow for flexibility when considering where you may receive care. With this option, if you, your health care provider, and the insurance company all agree, you may choose to receive your care in a nursing facility, at home, or in another care setting such as an adult day care center, an adult day health care facility, or an assisted-living center.

Guideline: Look for policies that offer and mention these provisions so you can be prepared to meet any future needs in a way that allows you and your health care provider as many options as possible.

SPOUSAL DISCOUNT

Many companies offer a 10 percent to 15 percent discount on premiums to couples who are covered together by the same company.

Guideline: If you and your spouse are considering LTC policies, whether purchased at the same time or a few years apart, look for a policy that offers the spousal discount.

GATEKEEPERS

This term can be alternately used with *qualifiers*. For the LTC policy to begin paying benefits, you must qualify for these benefits. To qualify, you must get through certain gatekeepers, meet certain standards. The most common of these are:

- Medical necessity. A physician says you need the care and requests it.
- Cognitive impairment. You need supervision to take care of yourself, as with Alzheimer's disease.

- Activities of daily living (ADLs). When you cannot perform two of the six ADLs; these include bathing, feeding, dressing, transferring, continence, and going to the toilet.

Guideline: If you want your policy to be tax qualified, then you will need to purchase a policy that does not offer medical necessity as a gatekeeper. However, if your premiums would not be tax qualified anyway because they do not meet the 7.5 percent of your Adjusted Gross Income limitation, then look for a policy that offers all three of these gatekeepers, where any one of them will allow you to qualify to receive benefits. Ask to see a specimen policy that defines the gatekeepers as well as the ADLs. Definitions for qualifications vary from company to company.

THE PREMIUM

This will be the amount you pay for your policy. It will depend on which insurance company you choose, which of the previous options you select, and your age and health at the time of purchase. You should be given a choice as to how you would like to pay your premiums: monthly, quarterly, semiannually, or annually.

Guideline: Try to pay on an annual basis. Some companies charge you more if you pay any other way. Calculate how much the other payment options would total for the year, and compare that to the total amount of the premium were you to pay annually.

GROUP OR INDIVIDUAL PLAN

Be sure to find out if the policy you are planning to purchase is with a group or is an individual LTC policy. There are significant differences between the two.

An individual plan. In this case, the insurance company has a written contract between you, the insured or policyholder, and them. You will receive a copy of the contract policy, and the company cannot make any changes to this policy without your consent.

A group plan. The insurance company agrees to provide you, the insured, with coverage and list you on a certificate of insurance you will receive. The *policyholder*, however, is a third party—your employer, a consumer group, or association. Thus the insurance company and the policyholder can agree to changes in the policy or contract, or *even cancel the policy*, without your approval. Your certificate of insurance summarizes the important provisions in the contract (or master policy). This certificate, however, is not the contract.

Most employers offer group plans for ease of administration. With most of these group plans there is little flexibility in benefits provided; longer elimination periods; limited benefit periods; poor inflation protection; no spousal discounts and, depending on the state, some are not guaranteed renewable.

Guideline: If you are offered a group plan by your employer or association, check out the costs and benefits of an individual plan before making any decisions. Many people believe that group insurance premiums are cheaper and, therefore, a better buy. This may not always be the case. There are many excellent individual plans available for the same or lesser cost with superior coverage options. If you do purchase a group plan, make sure it can be converted into an individual plan should you leave the group.

GUARANTEED RENEWABLE CLAUSE

Simply stated, the insurance company agrees to insure you for life as long as you pay the premium within the agreed-upon time frame.

Guideline: Purchase only a plan that is guaranteed renewable every year for the rest of your life. This is especially important if you buy a group plan.

THE COST OF A LONG-TERM-CARE POLICY

When purchasing a long-term-care policy, your annual premium is based on your age and health at the time of purchase. From that point on, the premiums should remain stable. For example, let's take a policy with the following benefits:

Benefit period	Lifetime
Benefit amount	$100 a day
Inflation option	5% compounded
Elimination period	0 day
Home health care	2 years at $50 a day

Table A gives an approximate yearly cost. Factors of age, the company you buy the policy from, and your health could change these rates.

TABLE A	
Age at Time of Purchase	**Yearly Premium per Person**
45–49	$ 746
50–54	$ 954
55–59	$1,255
60–64	$1,719
65	$2,580
70	$3,723
75	$6,734

Two points are noteworthy concerning policy costs:

1. If and when you use the benefits of certain LTC policies, your premium payments will cease.
2. With most LTC policies there can be a change in premium level if there is an across-the-board increase for all insured within the state, region, or county who have this particular plan.

SOME OFTEN-ASKED QUESTIONS ON COSTS

Here is a statistic I use a lot and will mention again because it is important that everyone see the possibility of long-term-care and the need to plan with insurance: Currently the average age of someone entering a nursing home is 84 years and the average stay is 2.9 years.

Question 1: Since I will probably not use this policy for years to come, is it better to wait and purchase a policy when I am older than to purchase one now and have to pay the annual premium for all these years?

Answer: In most cases, the earlier you buy a policy, the better. Using the following chart, find your approximate age to show you how much an LTC policy would cost, with premiums remaining stable, if you entered a nursing home at age eighty-four.

As you can see, the older you are at the time of purchase, the more it will cost you to have a policy. Remember also that you must be healthy at the time of purchase. The longer you wait, not only will a policy cost more, but also the greater the likelihood that you may not even be eligible due to failed health.

Question 2: Which is actually more expensive, the total cost of a policy, which I may never use, or the cost of a nursing home stay?

Answer: A nursing home stay.

Again, we'll use age eighty-four as entry into a nurs-

TABLE B			
Age at Purchase	Yearly Premium	Years Until Age 84	Total Cost of Premiums Paid
45	$ 746	39	$29,094
50	$ 954	34	$32,436
55	$1,255	29	$36,395
60	$1,719	24	$41,256
65	$2,580	19	$49,020
70	$3,723	14	$52,122
75	$6,734	9	$60,606

ing home as an example. In Table C, find the number of years you have before you turn eighty-four. So, if you are fifty-five years old today, look at the line for year thirty. This figure will indicate the projected yearly cost of a nursing home visit. Write that figure here _____ . As in our example, fifty-five years old, this figure is $148,176.

Compare this figure to the approximate total cost of a long-term-care policy as shown on Table B. Write this figure here _____ . At fifty-five this will be $36,395. Look at the difference in these two figures! It's a lot more expensive to pay $148,176 a year (about $12,000 a month) for a nursing home than $36,395 for the total cost of the long-term-care policy.

In all cases, the total cost of a long-term-care policy is far less expensive than the cost of one year in a nursing home.

Here is the cost per year of a nursing home over the next thirty years, assuming an annual inflation rate of 5 percent:

	TABLE C		
Year	Nursing Home Cost per Year	Year	Nursing Home Cost per Year
1	$36,000	16	$ 74,844
2	$37,800	17	$ 78,586
3	$39,690	18	$ 82,517
4	$41,681	19	$ 86,638
5	$43,760	20	$ 90,972
6	$45,953	21	$ 95,521
7	$48,245	22	$100,296
8	$50,652	23	$105,310
9	$53,185	24	$110,578
10	$55,843	25	$116,109
11	$58,640	26	$121,918
12	$61,576	27	$128,003
13	$64,651	28	$134,404
14	$67,889	29	$141,120
15	$71,278	30	$148,176

The following table demonstrates the advantages of 5 percent compounded interest over 5 percent simple interest or no inflation rider on a beginning daily benefit amount of $100.

BUYER'S CHECKLIST

Aside from the factors we have mentioned, everyone has a unique situation when it comes to purchasing insurance. This buyer's checklist is meant only as a reference. It is always important when you are about to make the commitment to spend money to protect yourself that you consult with your financial advisor and have a personalized plan created for you.

| | | | TABLE D | | | | |
Year	No Inflation Rider	5% Simple Interest	5% Compound Interest	Year	No Inflation Rider	5% Simple Interest	5% Compound Interest
1	$100	$100	$100	21	$100	$200	$265
2	$100	$105	$105	22	$100	$205	$27,8
3	$100	$110	$110	23	$100	$210	$292
4	$100	$115	$116	24	$100	$215	$307
5	$100	$120	$122	25	$100	$220	$322
6	$100	$125	$128	26	$100	$225	$338
7	$100	$130	$134	27	$100	$230	$355
8	$100	$135	$141	28	$100	$235	$373
9	$100	$140	$148	29	$100	$240	$392
10	$100	$145	$155	30	$100	$245	$412
11	$100	$150	$163	31	$100	$250	$433
12	$100	$155	$171	32	$100	$255	$455
13	$100	$160	$180	33	$100	$260	$478
14	$100	$165	$189	34	$100	$265	$502
15	$100	$170	$198	35	$100	$270	$527
16	$100	$175	$208	36	$100	$275	$553
17	$100	$180	$218	37	$100	$280	$581
18	$100	$185	$229	38	$100	$285	$610
19	$100	$190	$240	39	$100	$290	$641
20	$100	$195	$252	40	$100	$295	$673

Before you purchase a policy, however, be sure you will be able to afford these premiums for the rest of your life or until the benefits are used. It makes no sense to purchase an LTC policy while you are younger and able to afford it knowing that your retirement income will not cover the costs.

Guideline: Spend no more than 5 percent of your monthly income on premiums.

FINDING AN INSURANCE COMPANY

• Purchase a plan from a company that has a track record in providing LTC insurance *and in paying claims.* Look for a minimum of ten years of experience with this product.

• Purchase a plan from a company that is judged or rated financially sound by at least two of the following four independent rating services. The only acceptable ratings by these services are as follows:

A. M. Best	A++
Standard & Poor's	AA or better
Moody's	Aa or better
Duff & Phelps	AA or better

Check out several companies (and agents) before you buy. Be sure to compare benefits, coverage limitations, policy exclusions, and premiums.

FINDING THE RIGHT PLAN

Look for a plan that has these qualifications (use this as your checklist):

_____ Does not require a stay in a hospital as a precondition for benefits to begin. Most policies should no longer have this limitation, but it is still a good idea to check your prospective policy. _____ Covers care at home as well as in an institution.

_____ Does not require home health care to be administered by a professional health care worker or from a certified home health care agency; otherwise your benefits may not be paid.

_____ Covers custodial or "personal care" as well as intermediate care.

_____ Covers adult day care.

_____ Does not exclude preexisting conditions, or at least for not more than six months.

_____ Once you begin to receive benefits after a maximum time limit of ninety days, including the elimination period, you no longer have to pay premiums until you are up and on your own again.

_____ You have to satisfy the elimination period only once, no matter how many times you may need care.

_____ There is no change in premium level unless it is an across-the-board increase for all insured within the state, region, or county who carry the plan.

_____ Is guaranteed renewable. In some states, including California, all plans, including group plans, must be guaranteed renewable.

_____ Offers a grace period, keeping your policy in effect, in case you forget to make a premium payment.

_____ An agent should give you an "Outline of Coverage," a document, required by law, that summarizes important plan features. You do not have to complete an application or provide personal data to get one. Do not work with an agent who or company that is unwilling to supply one or disputes your right to have one.

_____ Compare "Outlines of Coverage" for all plans you are considering.

_____ Make sure that the policy you are about to purchase qualifies as a tax-deductible policy.

_____ Never pay cash to an agent. Write a check payable to the insurance company.

_____ Do not deal with an agent who pressures you into buying a policy. Take your time and do your homework.

_____ You have a "free look" period in which to review your policy. If you decide you do not want the policy after you have purchased it, you can cancel the policy and get your money back if you notify the company within the allowed time frame after the policy has been delivered.

_____ Pays your nursing home stay on an indemnity

basis, not on a reimbursement basis. Indemnity means that if your benefit amount is $200 a day but the actual cost of the nursing home is $150 a day, you still receive the entire $200. Reimbursement means that the company will only reimburse you for what you actually spend.

_____ If you purchase anything other than a lifetime benefit period, make sure that your policy has a feature called "restoration of benefits." If you recover and leave the nursing home, and are not readmitted for at least 180 consecutive days, with restoration of benefits the company will restore your original full benefit period.

_____ Your medical history is critical. Be sure to give correct information; otherwise the company can refuse to pay your claim for benefits or cancel your policy.

_____ To insure that no disagreements arise over the date you received your policy, either keep the envelope the policy came in, or insist that the agent gives you a signed and dated receipt when he or she delivers the policy.

_____ Ask a professional advisor about all the terms and conditions mentioned above that you do not understand. That individual has an obligation to answer your questions and to make sure you understand all the ramifications of the policy. The agent should assist you with the following:

- determining if LTC insurance is appropriate for you;
- selecting the company, policy options, and premiums that are best for your particular situation and needs;
- assisting you in filling out all the applications and necessary forms;
- submitting the policy for you and making sure the policy is issued correctly;
- monitoring any changes in the tax laws or federal legislation affecting LTC insurance, and keeping you informed.

For additional information or questions concerning long-term-care insurance, write or contact these organizations:

National Council on Aging
409 3rd Street, SW
Suite 200
Washington, DC 20024
Tel.: 202-479-1200

Health Insurance Association of America
1001 Pennsylvania Avenue, NW
Washington, DC 20004-2599
Hot line: 800-942-4242

To check the safety ratings of the companies you are interested in, call any of the following rating services:

A. M. Best	908-439-2200
Duff & Phelps	312-263-2610
Moody's	212-553-0377
Standard & Poor's	212-208-8000

chapter 6

Early Retirement

Retirement doesn't necessarily mean sixty-five anymore. Retirement now can mean fifty to fifty-five years of age, *when you could be offered early retirement!*

Author's note: For purposes of this chapter, "pension" is defined as a designated amount of money your company will give you each month for the rest of your retired life; and "qualified retirement plan" is defined as money (the majority of which are pretax funds) that has been put aside by you and/or the company and that can be accessed or completely withdrawn by you.

Doug and Shirley's Story

DOUG WORKED for a large company for twenty-eight years. The company was his entire life. The unit he supervised did "materials" inspections on operating plant components. Should some flaw have gone undetected, it could have been catastrophic. He felt his job would always be there as long as he maintained the level of performance they expected. He even received a commendation from the company president regarding a particular process he helped to invent that would save the company $2.5 million over a five-year period. Everything seemed to be going along well. But when suddenly struck with the dilemma of an early retirement decision, Doug and Shirley began to ride an emotional and financial roller coaster.

Doug: I couldn't believe I was being made to retire early. The news hit me broadside. Emotionally I had to deal with the end of a career. It felt like rejection, divorce. Most people who are career folk like myself believe in the "company." It's a marriage for life. This idea went to hell in a few short weeks. It was like being instantly homeless—out on the streets. One day I'm receiving a salary of $70,000 and the next day there would be less than half that amount— a pension of $27,000.

Shirley: Ten years ago, when Doug was forty-one, he thought about retiring at fifty-five. But our daughter would just be getting out of high school then and we realistically knew he wouldn't be able to retire before he was sixty. *We never expected Doug to be a target for retirement at fifty-one.*

Doug: Word got around late March through the company's E-mail (the computer network message system). One morning I turned on my machine and saw: *Targeted: twelve hundred people for early retirement. Qualifying factors: fifty years old and fifteen years of service.* It read like impending disaster. In my gut I knew they were talking about me. One week later, I received the official package marked "Voluntary Retirement Incentive," and I had one month to decide whether to accept the offer. I was given four weeks in which to plan the rest of my life. I know people who take more time than that to plan a vacation!

Shirley: Suddenly being faced with an income reduction of $40,000 a year meant that, aside from Doug having to find another job, I might also have to go back to work to supplement our income. The thought of giving up my volunteer work, changing my entire life at forty-five, and finding a job after having been away from the workplace for so many years was devastating. What was worse, I didn't even know where to begin.

Doug: Even though the company indicated it was a voluntary retirement, I knew they were downsizing. I could stay on, but there was a likelihood that the job wouldn't exist down the road. I could be fired without any of the benefits they offered in the early retirement package. That prospect was even more frightening. I felt I had no choice. All I could think about was how I would provide for my family.

Shirley: I worried that if Doug chose early retirement, we would have to make enormous changes to our lifestyle to survive financially. We couldn't make it on Doug's pension alone. Without Doug's salary we didn't know how we would pay for our daughter's education. You see, aside from putting money in Doug's 401K plan for the past twenty-eight years, we couldn't save any other money. Fortunately, we had always been careful about how we spent our money and lived fairly frugally, so we have no debts except for our mortgage.

Doug: I spent the first two weeks incapable of making a decision. I ran around in circles literally burning a hole in the carpet. All I could think about was that I would have to pursue reemployment aggressively. At my age it wasn't going to be easy. Mentally I equated it with being married for twenty-eight years and suddenly having to find a new wife. I've never been so terrified in my life.

What was I going to do? Even though I had $220,000 saved in my 401K plan, I was told I couldn't touch those funds until I turned 59½ without paying a penalty. With only two weeks left before I had to make a decision, we were desperate for help.

Discussion

Companies are presenting early retirement options because they must change with the changing economy. So they are providing the best deals possible as entice-

ment for people like Doug to retire earlier than anticipated. Commonly, the inducement includes an **increased pension amount** and the **receipt of that
pension immediately.** This monthly pension amount
is usually more than you would be entitled to if you
stayed with the company another three to five years.
So the question that arises is, "Why continue to work
for less money later?" Other benefits offered may include health care and anything else the company feels
might aid your ability to retire.

Another form of early retirement offering may be
a lump sum settlement in the form of severance pay.
If this is the case, your company pension usually does
not begin prior to age fifty-five, so the severance
amount will help get you through this lag period.

To determine if you can accept an early retirement
offer, follow the steps in the Guidelines section. Your
current financial situation will be the determining factor for your early retirement outlook, but the information and advice you get along the way will be equally
important.

Doug and Shirley didn't have access to correct and
consistent information. They really didn't know what
their financial alternatives were. Doug was told by a
financial advisor that he could not touch his 401K savings ($220,000) until he turned 59½ years of age with-
out a penalty. The basis for this belief is that the
majority of funds in retirement accounts* contain pretax money that is set aside for retirement. By law you
cannot access these accounts before age 59½ without
incurring a 10 percent federal penalty tax. The reason
for the penalty is that the government wants to make

---

*For definition and discussion of 401K, IRA, SEP/IRA, KEOGH, tax-shel-
tered annuity, profit-sharing plan, pension plan, defined benefit pension
plan, and IRA rollover, see the Glossary.

sure the money remains in these accounts and is used to support you during your retirement years. However, what the financial advisor did not know was that, with the massive onset of early retirements, legislation was passed in 1986 that *does allow* access to these funds prior to age 59½ in *any or all* of your retirement accounts without sustaining this 10 percent penalty tax from the federal government (as well as an additional state penalty*). The method that allows anyone access to qualified retirement plan money, whether retiring or not,† before they are 59½ years old, and without penalties, is known as substantially equal periodic payments (SEPP). The IRS code that cites this method is Section 72(t)(2)(A)(iv).

Here's how substantially equal periodic payments work:

HOW LONG MUST YOU TAKE SEPP?

You must take substantially equal amounts of money from your account annually for five years or until you are 59½, *whichever is longer.* For instance, Doug is only fifty-one, so he must take designated or equal amounts of money each year from his retirement account until he is 59½. That's eight years. If Doug had been fifty-six and started to receive money under the SEPP system, he would have to take his payments for the full five years until he was 61. Remember, the rule for SEPP is five years or until you are 59½, whichever is longer.

---

*This penalty will vary from state to state. Confer with your financial advisor or tax consultant for the amount.

†If you are not retiring, however, most companies have rules that will not allow you to withdraw these funds early.

HOW MUCH MONEY CAN YOU TAKE?

Now that you know how long you must take to withdraw your money to avoid penalties, the question becomes, "How much can you get from your retirement account?" There are three methods the IRS uses to calculate substantially equal periodic payments: life expectancy, amortization, and annuity. The amount will differ for each person based on which method an individual chooses and the following factors:

1. Your life expectancy and/or your wife's life expectancy (based on an IRS life expectancy table);
2. The amount in your retirement account;
3. An estimated interest rate for investment returns.

Once you have determined how much you will be receiving annually based on one of the above methods, those amounts cannot be changed. Doug chose the amortization method and, based on his particular factors, he *must* withdraw $15,400 a year—no more and no less.

You will undoubtedly need help from a financial advisor to select the SEPP method that best suits your particular situation.

There are two possible snags to be aware of with substantially equal periodic payments. If you do not use a financial advisor who is familiar with SEPP, you could run into these problems:

HOW YOUR MONEY IS DISTRIBUTED

For example, calculations are made for your SEPP and you have to withdraw $12,000 a year. You retire in

TIP:

Have the firm that will be calculating your SEPP state on the company letterhead (not the financial advisor's letterhead) that the company is responsible for calculating your substantially equal periodic payments and will be responsible for any mistakes and any penalty incurred.

June and receive $6,000 for the period between June and December. The following year, though, you will receive the full $12,000. At some future date, the IRS could determine that the year you received $6,000 is not an equal payment to the annual amount of $12,000 you should be getting and penalize you for all monies received to that point. What can you do?

1. Make sure that the firm distributing your SEPP gives you the additional amount from the principal ($6,000) that first year so you have received your entire annual SEPP amount.

or

2. Wait until January 1 to begin to take your SEPP (remember, you can begin SEPP anytime you wish; you are just required to continue to receive SEPP for five years or until you are 59½, whichever is longer).

or

3. Select investments, such as an annuity, that fall under certain rulings that even though the first years' distribution amount varies from the other years, because the monthly amounts are identical and cannot change, they meet the rules of SEPP.

The following is a good example of a guarantee from a major company:

_____ Company is willing to assume responsibility for making accurate calculations and distributions under the substantially equal periodic payment regulations of the IRS. By complying with these regulations, the retiree may receive a stream of payments prior to age 59½ without incurring the usual 10 percent premature tax penalty. We will work with you and the client to set up a distribution method that best fits the client's needs and fits all of the IRS regulations. For that portion of the retiree's funds that are entrusted to us, we will certify that if we make any errors in the calculation that result in any tax penalties being assessed, we will pay those charges.

HOW YOUR MONEY IS INVESTED

This is especially significant under SEPP. For instance, Doug chose the amortization method and must take 7 percent of his funds each year to qualify for SEPP. Let's say Doug's advisor had him invest all of his money in mutual funds for growth with the idea that the mandatory 7 percent SEPP would be withdrawn from that growth at the end of the year. That very year, rather than the funds increasing in value, they *decreased* by just 10 percent. Doug is still required to withdraw the 7 percent for his SEPP. Since there is no growth now, that money must come from the principal. The account has now been depleted 17 percent (that's 10 percent in loss of principal and another 7 percent for SEPP). To make up for that loss, Doug's account will have to increase 20.5 percent in value next year to break even, plus another 7 percent for the following year's SEPP. That's a 27.5 percent increase in one year!

Remember, when something goes from 2 to 1, it decreases by 50 percent. For it to go from 1 to 2 is a 100 percent increase! So a 50 percent decrease needs a 100 percent increase to get back even.

HOW TO INVEST FOR SEPP

A good rule to follow when investing for SEPP: Invest at least 70 percent of your funds safely for income (not growth).

There is a very good chance that over the five years or more than you are required to take SEPP, there

TIP:

Under all circumstances, it is extremely important that you only deal with an advisor who is knowledgeable in the area of SEPP. To make sure the financial advisor you are working with is savvy, use this test for prospective advisors: Ask which of the three SEPP methods will provide the greatest amount of income. Their immediate reply should be the amortization method with a single life expectancy factor. If the answer isn't on the tip of their tongue, you know they are not familiar with SEPP. (Don't bother asking the question if you see a copy of this book on their shelf!)

could be a downturn in the markets. Wait until SEPP is over and then you can invest more toward growth if you want. For instance: If Doug was not taking SEPP and the funds decreased by 10 percent, since he does not have to take that 7 percent SEPP payment this year or next, the funds have to grow only 20 percent for him to be even. There is a big difference between 20 percent and 41 percent.

Given that most advisors are not familiar with SEPP, they will probably suggest a method called annuitization (see page 152) to avoid the 10 percent penalty. The use of the annuitization is not recommended for this purpose. SEPP offers greater advantages in most cases.

THE "FIFTY-FIVE OR OVER" RULE

Substantially equal periodic payments and annuitization are not the only ways to access your money without penalty before 59½ in a qualified retirement plan like Doug's (401K). Age will be a factor in determining what you can and cannot do. Your choices will differ if you are *over* or *under* fifty-five years of age in the year in which you separate from service or retire.

If you are fifty-five years of age or older in the year of your retirement, you can withdraw any or all the money, whenever you wish, from your qualified retirement plan without any penalties whatsoever. If Doug had been fifty-five or older in the year his retirement began, he could have accessed the $220,000 in his 401K anytime he wished and in any amount he wanted, without worry of penalties (federal and state). He would not be limited to the $15,400 a year that he must take under SEPP until he is 59½. The key is to be fifty-five or older anytime during the year you retire. For example, if Doug's retirement began in April and his fifty-fifth birthday wasn't until December 31 of that year, he would qualify. This rule of "fifty-five and over" pertains only to money in employee qualified plans, not for any other retirement account, such as an IRA, an IRA rollover, or SEP/IRA.

WARNING

- If you are 55 or older and transfer your funds from your qualified plan into an IRA rollover, you will also transfer away the right to access these funds at your convenience without penalty until you turn 59½ unless you take substantially equal periodic payments.
- If you are not or will not be fifty-five in the year of your retirement, like Doug, who was only fifty-one, the best way to avoid penalties, if you need to access those funds, is by rolling over your funds into an IRA rollover and taking substantially equal periodic payments.

If you are presented with an early retirement offer, the following guidelines will help you in deciding if you can retire.

Guidelines

For many working people, the prospect of early retirement will be one of the hardest decisions to make. The considerations are numerous and, as in Doug's case, will have to be reconciled in a fairly short time. Carefully taking stock of the emotional and financial consequences of an offered early retirement becomes essential because they will generally differ from an anticipated and planned retirement.

To understand whether you are financially ready to retire early, you may want to seek advice from a financial professional. In fact, when a company offers an early retirement incentive, the word gets out quickly and you will undoubtedly have financial advisors beat-

TIP:

If you are taking early retirement because your spouse or partner's earnings cover your financial needs and you are dependent on those earnings, you should consider purchasing a "level term"* life insurance policy on him or her to protect you in case anything happens to your spouse or partner if he or she is not already adequately insured. See Chapter Seven, page 154.

ing a path to your door. Before selecting an advisor, prepare yourself by reading Chapter One.

The following questions, guidelines, and formulas, whether used by yourself in making the decision, or in conjunction with an advisor, will help determine if you can retire, what your financial needs will be, and if you can meet them.

ASSESSING THE SITUATION

Carefully evaluate your immediate situation and your long-range plans in the following areas of concern.

YOUR EMOTIONAL QUOTIENT

- At what age were you really planning to retire? Was it fewer than five years from now?
- If you could afford to, would you retire now?
- Are you ready to give up the daily work routine?
- Does your spouse want you to stop working?
- Would you like to be doing some other job besides the one you are now doing?
- What is the outlook of your company's future? Are they permanently reducing their workforce to cut expenses?
- If you don't accept the early retirement offering, could you be fired or relocated? Will your workload be increased? Will you be demoted? Will your salary be reduced?

An answer of "no" to most of these questions suggests you aren't ready for retirement. Either stay where

---

*You will need the policy only for the number of years your spouse or partner plans to work. If he or she will retire in ten years, take out a ten-year policy.

you are or secure another income-producing opportunity elsewhere. Be sure, however, you continue con-
tributing the maximum allowed to any or all retirement
savings accounts.

A "yes" to the majority of these questions makes
you a likely candidate for taking early retirement. Your
next considerations will be financial and will confirm
or contradict your ability to retire comfortably.

THE FINANCIAL FACTORS

Do you have money set aside for these eventualities?

Spousal Income

- Does your spouse or partner work? If you
  count on his or her income, how much longer
  will he or she be willing to work?
- Is there a possibility that this person, too, may
  be presented with an early retirement offer,
  or lose his or her job?
- Could you make it financially without the second income?

Children and Education

- Do you still have children in school?
- Will this early retirement affect your ability
  to pay for their education?
- Can you ask your children to pay for part or
  all of their education?

Parents

- Will you be financially responsible for an elderly parent in the future?
- Are you going to inherit any money?*

---

*Make sure these funds are coming to you via a trust. See Chapter Two,
on trusts and wills.

Your Home

- Are you planning to sell your home? Is it a good time to be selling?
- Will you buy a new home? Is it a good time to be buying?
- Does your home need immediate or foreseeable repairs, such as a new roof? Do you already have money set aside for these repairs?

Life's Little (and Not So Little) Luxuries

- How is your car holding up? Does it require a lot of repairs? When will you be needing or wanting a new car?
- Do you like to travel? Is this something you planned to do during retirement?
- What other luxury items did you have your heart set on? A boat? A motor home? Will you still be able to afford them? Can you live without them?

Health Care

- Will your company be passing on part of your health insurance costs to you now or in the future?
- When you turn sixty-five, will the company discontinue health insurance for your spouse?
- Do you have a durable power of attorney for health care (see Chapter Four) or long-term-care insurance (see Chapter Five)? Now is the time to put things in order, not later, when the unforeseen could be very costly.
- Will you now be responsible for your own dental and optical care? If dental and optical care are not part of the retirement plan, you

will be offered the opportunity to continue coverage for the next eighteen months under COBRA (the Consolidated Omnibus Budget Reconciliation Act of 1985). Here's how it may work. A dental plan under COBRA may cost a couple $58 a month. Along with this premium, you may be required to copay 20 percent or more for any work done. Let's look at whether it is a worthwhile investment. During the year you and your spouse have two cleanings each at $50 each ($200), X rays at $80 each ($160), and you have a crown replaced for $350. Your total expenditure is $710. If you choose COBRA, your costs would be $58 a month ($696), and 20 percent of the dental bills (142). You have now paid $838 for the year. That's $128 more than paying these dental expenses directly. You may be better off paying for these services directly, and not taking COBRA, unless you have poor teeth and eyes requiring constant care. Rule of thumb: If you think you will need more than $900 a year in dental work, take advantage of COBRA. Otherwise put about $60 a month away to cover dental expenses when they arise.

TIP:

Most early retirement health benefit offers will not include dental or optical care. If your company now covers these two and if early retirement is in the air, get all your dental and optical work completed beforehand.

INFORMATION-GATHERING

This next step is to look at your present financial status. To help determine whether you are able to retire from a financial standpoint, you need to do some information-gathering about your expenses and income.

CALCULATING YOUR MONTHLY EXPENSES

A crucial part of your retirement decision will mean figuring out how much it really costs to live each month—not what you think it costs you, but an accountability of every penny you spend. Often people will tell me that they bring home $3,000 a month, so it must cost them $3,000 a month to live. But what about those expenses that occur sporadically throughout the year, such as clothing, vacations, car maintenance and registration, and gifts? Necessities or not, they have to be paid for, too. So an accurate picture of what you need to live on is essential. The following list will provide you with working categories.

The procedure

1. Go through your checkbook month by month for one full year.
2. Assign a category for each check and add each category separately. For example, add all your "electric" payments for the past year.
3. Divide each category total by 12 to get an average monthly payment. For example, total electric, $960 ÷ 12 = $80 per month average payment.
4. Plug each average monthly payment into the list provided. If there is no category provided for some of your expenditures, place them under "additional," or create your own category.

MONTHLY EXPENSE LIST

Regular Monthly Expenses		Other Expenses	
Mortgage	_____	Property taxes	_____
Equity loan	_____	Homeowners' ins.	_____
Condo fees	_____	House maint.	_____
Utilities	_____	Pet food	_____
Garbage	_____	Vet. bills	_____
Phone	_____	Car insurance	_____
Water	_____	DMV registration	_____
Food	_____	Car maintenance	_____
Car payments	_____	Makeup	_____
Gasoline	_____	Clothes	_____
Haircuts	_____	Shoes	_____
Credit cards	_____	Jewelry	_____
Alimony	_____	Dental	_____
Child support	_____	Optical	_____
Cable TV	_____	Medicine	_____
Video rentals	_____	Health/LTC ins.	_____
Entertainment	_____	Tax prep.	_____
Club fees	_____	Legal advice	_____
Donations	_____	Tolls/parking	_____
Lottery	_____	Sports	_____
Liquor	_____	Golf fees	_____
Diet program	_____	Golf balls/shoes	_____
Cash on hand	_____	Vacations	_____
Restaurants	_____	Gifts	_____
Manicures	_____	Books	_____
Facials	_____	Subscriptions	_____
Dry cleaning	_____	Gardening	_____

TIPS:

1. **Don't skimp on your expenses.** *Don't forget to include dental or optical expenses, once covered by the company plan but that you may now be responsible for. Being shortsighted may mean not having enough to live on now or in the future.*

2. **Don't double-expense yourself.** *If you take out $500 in cash and spend it on groceries, dining out, or gasoline, be sure not to place that amount in these categories as well as in the cash category. You will find your expenses overinflated.*

3. *When you deposit your paychecks "less cash," this will not appear in any records. Be sure to account for that money in your expenses.*

Life insurance	____	Licenses (hunt./ fish.)	____
Cigarettes	____	Tackle/ammunition	____
Bottled water	____	Pest control	____
Housecleaning	____	Hobbies	____
Bank fees	____	Firewood	____
Cellular phone	____	Education	____
Time-share fees	____	Pool/spa	____
Vitamins	____	Burial plots	____
Misc.	____	AAA fees/payments	____

Total all monthly expenses $ ____ (E)

YOUR INCOME

Gathering all current sources of monthly income will determine whether you have enough to cover your expenses. Approach each figure with long-term solutions in mind, not quick fixes. How long will these sources of income continue? Include those that will continue at least three years. If your spouse will be retiring in six months, do not include "spouse's current employment income" on the list. Or if you plan to sell a rental property to pay off a debt, don't include a figure for "rental income." At this point don't include potential income from your retirement accounts.

Your pension income	____
Spouse/partner's pension income	____
Spouse/partner's current employment income	____
Interest income	____
Bond income	____
Dividend income	____
Rental Income	____

TIP:

Other business income   _____

Misc. income   _____

Social Security income   _____

Disability income (if long term)   _____

Spouse/partner's unemployment income   _____

Loan repayments (if long term)   _____

Limited partnership income   _____

　　　　　　Total all monthly income $_____(F)

*At age 70½ you are re-quired to start with-drawing funds if you have not already done so.

Calculating the outcome

Subtract your total expenses (line E) from your total income (line F):

Total Monthly Income   (F) $ _____

Total Monthly Expenses   (E) $ _____

Monthly excess or deficit   =   ± _____(G)

A zero or a positive figure (excess) indicates that you currently have enough income to cover your expenses. If this is the case and you have money in retirement accounts, consider leaving the money in those retirement accounts to continue to grow, tax-deferred, until you need the money or must begin to withdraw it at 70½.* A negative figure (deficit) tells you how much money you must generate, after taxes from your retirement accounts, to cover your expenses. If you don't have any retirement accounts, the amount on line G tells you how much you will have to earn from another job.

YOUR RETIREMENT ACCOUNTS

Now let's look at your retirement accounts to see if you have enough money to retire. The formula is quite simple, as you will see when we use Doug as an example. Doug's previous calculations indicated he needed $400 a month more to meet his monthly expenses (G).

Total in Doug's retirement accounts	$220,000
Multiply by a conservative interest rate (6%)	× .06
	$ 13,200
Divide by 12 months	12
This is Doug's pretax monthly income	$ 1,100 (a)
Multiply by tax bracket (25%)	× .25
Tax payment	$ 275 (b)
Subtract (b) from (a) to get after-tax monthly income	$ 1,100 (a) −275 (b)
Doug's after-tax monthly income from his retirement account	$ 825
Subtract amount needed (G)	$ −400 (G)
Equals monthly excess (or deficit)	$ 425

Doug can retire. His retirement accounts generate $425 more a month than he needs. If you still don't have enough to cover expenses, see Chapter Eight, on minimizing expenses and maximizing income.* You may also need to begin looking for another job, preferably one that will allow you to begin saving money for when you cannot work anymore.

Like Doug, if you have a monthly excess, you have two choices:

1. Take the extra income now.
2. Invest the excess for growth.

For most of you, investing for growth will be important, especially if you are cutting it close. Years from now you may need more money due to inflation.

---

*Whether you are considering retirement or not and whether or not you can meet your financial needs, always consider minimizing your debts.

FREEZING THE SITUATION

This section is important only for those people, like Doug, who have decided they can take early retirement because they have enough money in their retirement plan to generate the interest they need to live on.

Once you have accepted the early retirement offer, you may not be able to change your mind. Most of you will continue to work for two to three months before you leave the company and begin retirement. After you retire, it could take the company an additional six weeks to distribute or "roll over" your funds. Together, it can be several months from the time you sign your early retirement papers until you begin receiving income from those funds. This is what I refer to as the "yield" time.

With the retirement income calculations done, the decision has been made to take early retirement based on the interest your retirement funds will generate. You will want to make sure that there is as much money in your retirement fund when you need it as there was when you made the original calculations. If your retirement plan is invested in either equity growth funds, stock and bond funds, bond funds, utility funds, or in your company's stock, it could fluctuate in value. This can be very dangerous. During the "yield" time you will want to ensure the safety of your funds by freezing your current situation until you have access to your money. *Move your funds into a safe, nonfluctuating, investment situation within your retirement plan until the "yield" time is over and you can invest those funds for your retirement income.* Most qualified plans have at least four or five different investment options for your money. These generally fall under the categories of conservative growth, aggressive growth, income, income and growth, or safety. If your plan does not offer an option with maximum safety, try to diversify your funds among as many categories as possible. The old adage "better safe than sorry" fits this situation. Following is an example of what could go wrong.

One of my clients, Bill, signed his retirement papers and was going to continue to work until his retirement day two months later. During this time, against my advice, he left his money in various equity growth funds that had been performing extremely well. He did this because he wanted to get as much money out of this account as he could. One month later, however, the market took a significant downturn, carrying Bill's funds with it. Bill no longer had enough principal to generate the amount of income he needed for his retirement. But he had already signed the papers and had no recourse. This happened in October 1987, when many unhappy retirees had their retirement accounts in equity growth funds and the stock market went down more than 500 points in just one day! If you think this is an unlikely scenario, it is not! Consider what happened to IBM in 1993. Consistently a secure stock, it went from $86 a share to the low $40s in months. Those who worked for IBM and had their retirement account invested in IBM stock saw the value of their account cut in half.

WHAT TO DO WITH THE MONEY FROM YOUR RETIREMENT PLAN

At some point you will have to decide what you are going to do with your retirement funds. These are the choices of where you can place your money when you retire:

1. Your company may allow you to keep any or all of your money right where it is—in the company plan.
2. You can take all the money and do a rollover with it.
3. If permitted to leave money in the company plan, you can keep some there and do a partial IRA rollover with any amount you choose.
4. You can do as many rollovers as you want and have them in as many places as you want.
5. You may withdraw all or any portion of your funds and simply pay ordinary income taxes on it.
6. You may roll over some of your funds, withdraw the rest, and pay ordinary income taxes on the amount withdrawn.
7. You may withdraw all the funds in one year and ten- or five-year-average your taxes *if you qualify*.

Numbers 5 and 6 apply only if you are 55 or older in the year of your retirement.

WHAT IS AN IRA ROLLOVER?

An IRA rollover is the means by which you can transfer the assets from one tax-deferred retirement fund, such as your company's qualified plan, to another. There are no tax consequences at the time of the transfer. As funds are withdrawn you are taxed on that specific amount as ordinary income during that year. This does not mean you may withdraw funds anytime you wish. By law you must be 59½ or older or you will incur a 10 percent penalty tax. This penalty is waived, however, if you choose to take substantially equal periodic payments. You must begin to withdraw the minimum required funds from your IRA rollover by April 1 of the year after you turn 70½. If you do not, a 50 percent penalty will be charged on the total amount that you should have withdrawn. An IRA rollover account can be opened in any of the following: banks, insurance companies, brokerage firms, discount brokerage firms, mutual fund companies, and credit unions.

What you need to know if you are the beneficiary of an IRA or IRA rollover: The rules that govern what you are allowed to do as a beneficiary of an IRA or IRA rollover are dictated by whether you were a spouse or nonspouse of the deceased individual who owned the account. The chart below briefly sums up those rules. They are complex enough, however, that we recommend you seek the expertise of a tax attorney or financial adviser.

Designated Beneficiary	Participant dies before required distribution date	Participant dies after required distribution date
Spouse	1. Minimum distributions postponed until *later* of: • year following participant's death. • year participant would have attained 70.5, or • end of the fifth year after the participant's death, if the plan permits and the surviving spouse elects. 2. Minimum distributions over spouse's life expectancy. 3. Rollover available; possible deferral to second generation. 4. May elect to defer excess accumulation tax.	1. Minimum distributions must continue *at least as rapidly* as during life of participant. If his/her life expectancy was being recalculated, distributions must continue over the spouse's single life expectancy. Otherwise, distributions continue to be distributed over the participant and spouse's joint life expectancy. 2. Rollover available. 3. May elect to defer excess accumulation tax.
Nonspouse individual	1. Minimum distributions over life of designated beneficiary beginning in year following death (otherwise, distributions must be completed by end of fifth year following participant's death). 2. Rollover not available.	1. Minimum distributions must continue *at least as rapidly* as during life of participant. If his/her life expectancy was being recalculated, distributions continue over the beneficiary's single life expectancy. Otherwise, distributions continue over the participant and beneficiary's joint life expectancy. 2. Rollover not available.

WHAT IS TEN- OR FIVE-YEAR AVERAGING

Ten-year averaging. If you were fifty years of age or older on January 1, 1986, you are entitled on a one-time basis to use ten-year averaging to pay taxes on funds received in a lump sum from your retirement

TIP:

If you and your spouse have set up a living trust (hold your assets in trust), make sure the primary beneficiary named on all your retirement accounts is the individual name of your spouse and not the trust. If you name the trust as the primary beneficiary, it will be subjected to the same rules as a nonspouse and the account will have to be wiped clean within five years. The trust should be named the contingent beneficiary only.

plan. The entire amount in the plan must be received within one taxable year, and you must have been an active participant in the plan for five or more taxable years before the year of distribution. This method of taxation is highly desirable for amounts of less than $400,000. As time marches on, fewer and fewer of us will be eligible for ten-year averaging. In fact, anyone born after 1936 is no longer eligible for this method of taxation. Why? you wonder. This method can save you from paying a lot of taxes over your lifetime, so the government has eliminated it.

Simply stated,* by dividing the total amount in your retirement fund by 10, taking this amount and looking up the tax figure on the 1986 individual tax rate table (even if you are married), and multiplying *this* tax figure by 10, you will find approximately what you owe. You will discover that the taxes you owe are significantly lower, based on a tax bracket of one tenth of the total amount, than if you were to withdraw all the funds and pay ordinary income taxes on the amount. For many, paying taxes via ten-year averaging will be significantly lower than the total amount of taxes you will eventually pay on your IRA rollover withdrawals.

Five-year averaging†. This method is available to anyone 59½ years of age or older on a one-time basis only. Again, the entire amount in the plan must be paid out within one taxable year, and you must have been an active participant in the plan for five or more taxable years before the year of distribution. The calculations are done exactly like ten-year averaging (you use the number 5 instead), except that you must use the cur-

---

*Do not use this formula for calculations. A qualified professional can help you make exact determinations for tax purposes.

†After the tax year 1999, five-year averaging for lump sum distributions will no longer be available.

rent year's individual tax table rate. This method is generally more desirable for amounts exceeding $400,000.

Spousal privilege. If you qualify to use either averaging method of taxation and you die before utilizing either of these methods, your spouse can continue to use ten- or five-year averaging for those funds even if that person does not qualify on his or her own.

CHOICES! CHOICES! CHOICES!

As you can see, there are many options for placing your money. All too often, people about to retire are told that they must roll over all of their retirement funds into one place. You do not! One hundred percent of your money does *not* have to be placed into one institution. You have choices. The two main choices—the IRA rollover and leaving your money in the company plan—provide advantages and disadvantages for the early retiree.

THE IRA ROLLOVER

Advantages:

1. Withholding tax. The IRS does not withhold 20 percent for taxes when a distribution is made.
2. Investment options. In most IRA rollovers you have unlimited choices in how to invest your money. You can choose from thousands of individual stocks, bonds, or mutual funds, just to name a few.
3. Investment flexibility. The numbers of transactions in most IRA rollovers are unlimited. You can trade as often and as many times as you wish.

4. Order entry. Orders to buy or sell can be placed over the telephone.
5. Order execution. When purchasing or selling an investment, your transactions usually are confirmed immediately.
6. Professional advice. You may be afforded the opportunity to have a personal advisor watching over your investments and telling you how best to invest your funds.

Disadvantages:

1. Taxation. IRA rollovers are not eligible for ten- or five-year averaging.
2. Accessibility. If you are under 59½, you can only access your money though SEPP or annuitization to avoid the 10 percent penalty.
3. Fees and commissions. There will be fees and commissions if you use a broker.
4. By April 1st of the year after you turn 70.5, you must begin withdrawals.

LEAVING YOUR MONEY IN THE COMPANY PLAN

Advantages:

1. Accessibility. If you are fifty-five or older in the year of retirement, the company plan allows you to withdraw funds without incurring the 10 percent penalty. You may withdraw funds as often as and in any amount you wish. You are not locked into fixed payments, as you would be in the SEPP method in an IRA rollover. As your monetary needs change, so can your income.
2. Fees and commissions. There are no fees or

commissions for most company plans, as there would be from a brokerage firm.

3. Taxation. If you qualify, this option offers the ability to do ten- or five-year averaging for taxation of the funds.

4. You do not have to start making mandatory withdrawals from your company plan by April 1st of the year after you turn 70½, *if you are still working.*

Disadvantages:

1. Investment options. Your investments are limited in the company plan. You may choose only among the funds it offers.

2. Investment flexibility. Many plans allow investment changes only once a quarter because of the extensive paperwork involved. Technology will do away with the "once in a quarter" rule and allow for a limitless number of transfers.

3. Order entry. Many plans require that you personally fill out an investment change form. More and more companies are able to offer this service by telephone.

4. Order execution. It often takes three to six weeks for the change to take place, sometimes resulting in missed opportunities or loss of funds. Technology will provide more immediate transfers. *Ask your company if they are planning to automate soon. If they are, it may be worth the wait.*

5. Withholding tax. When you do access the money in the plan, 20 percent will be held back for taxes. Since you will owe this money anyway, this is seemingly less of a disadvantage.

6. Professional advice. Within your retirement plan, you are solely responsible for deciding about how your funds are invested. Because you are already familiar with the investment options and their performances, you can readily manage your own money.

SUMMARY

Under 55: If you are under age 55 in the year of retirement, do an IRA rollover. The flexibility and investment options outweigh any reason to stay in the company plan. If a large sum of money is involved, consider dividing the rollovers between or among two or three different custodians (the place where your money is kept).

55 to 59½: Between ages 55 (in the year of retirement) and 59½, if the company allows, leave at least some money in the plan. In this way you will have total flexibility to access your money at any time and in any amount you want and still avoid the 10 percent penalty.

Over 59½: The choice is yours. If you think you will ten- or five-year-average your funds, or if at least you want to keep these options open, leave the money in the company plan. If you have no intention of averaging, an IRA rollover will offer you more investment possibilities. Again, if it is a large sum of money, consider diversifying between or among two or three different custodians.

ADVANTAGE AND DISADVANTAGE QUICK-REFERENCE TABLE		
Items	IRA Rollover	Company Plan
Investment options	Unlimited	Limited
Investment flexibility	Good	Limited
Order entry	Over the phone	In person or by phone
Order execution	Confirmed immediately	Possible waiting period
Taxation—10- and 5-year averaging	No	Yes
Accessibility	By SEPP under 59½ only	55 or older in year of retirement; under 55 by SEPP*
Fees and commissions	Yes	Usually not
Professional advice	Yes	Usually not
Mandatory withdrawals at 70.5	Yes	No†

*Not all company plans are set up to do SEPP.
†If you are still working you are allowed to maintain your funds in the plan regardless of your age.

WHEN DO YOU HAVE TO DECIDE WHAT TO DO WITH YOUR RETIREMENT MONEY?

The decision to take early retirement is stressful enough. Fortunately, you don't have to add to it by deciding immediately about what to do with your money. Many companies will allow you to keep your money in the company plan for one year after your retirement date. Most will allow you to keep your money in the company plan indefinitely.* Until you know exactly what you are going to do with your money, *don't rush into anything!* You have time to weigh your options and plan your strategies carefully.

*You must begin taking minimum distributions from your company plan by April 1st of the year after you turn 70½.

Shirley: The early retirement came as a blessing in disguise. Not only has Doug's work stress been alleviated, he also has come to realize that the world doesn't revolve around his job. Sure, his ego was bruised initially to think that his company may not need his services, but once he faced the fact that it was nothing personal, it was easier to accept. I once heard that no matter how high your position, leaving an impression when you leave a company is like taking your hand out of a bucket of water: Once the initial ripples subside, it's as if you were never there. So rather than viewing ourselves as victims of our times, shouldn't we look inside ourselves for our strength and talents to cope with our ever-changing world? Who knows? Along the way we may find we like ourselves better for our abilities to live more meaningful lives.

Joint and Survivor Benefits

chapter 7

Two can live as cheaply as one, but one can't live any less cheaply!

Anna's Story

Hank's retirement party seemed to last twenty years. We went to special occasions with family and friends, to holiday picnics, to the movies, and out to eat. Hank was always so busy around the house, too. He loved to build and fix things while I worked in my English garden. We were like kids again after all these years—not a care in the world.

He felt that if anything happened to him, I would have the house to keep me going and could always sell it if I needed to. Every time he said that, I always thought, "How silly of him. Why would I want to sell our house? Our son grew up here, it's paid for, and I can't imagine being comfortable in a strange place." Hank saw to it that our house was paid for by the time he retired and we were virtually debt-free. We were from the old school of thought, you know, and didn't believe in running up unnecessary bills.

Our household expenses were pretty much the same from month to month, so we were able to meet our expenses on our $1,385 a month. We did okay. We received two Social Security checks—$600 for Hank and $300 for me—and $500 from Hank's pension. Actually, the pension check came to $485 because his company deducted money for me to continue receiving after Hank was gone. I think that was part of his retirement plan, but we never really talked about it at the time. Hank took care of everything. He never really explained it to me, but he told me I'd get along just fine.

Everything came to a screeching halt when Hank died, though. All that time I thought everything would be okay, I never realized I would stop getting one Social Security check and would get only $243 from his pension. You might think that $842 a month is enough for one person, but a $543 drop in monthly income is a lot, especially when you still have to pay the electric bills, the tax on the property, and everything else. Rates on things like electricity and phone calls are so much higher today. I certainly think twice about turning on the air conditioning when it gets hot in the valley because it costs so much. I even sold our car. I wish I could have kept it, but gasoline is a luxury I just can't afford either. When I have to go into town to shop or visit my sister at the nursing home, I wait for a ride or take the bus. I have a senior discount pass for that.

The upkeep on the house is my biggest problem. It's older, and so am I. I simply can't maintain it by myself. Hank always took care of the big things around here. He was very handy that way, strong and energetic. Now, if something goes wrong, I have to wait for my nephew to visit to fix it or pay someone to take care of the problem. Goodness knows, I don't have any money for extras, much less emergencies. I even pulled out my beautiful garden to keep the water bills down. I just kept a little something for myself to putter around in—just to keep occupied.

I guess Hank and I didn't look far enough ahead. You just don't think about getting older and being alone. It does happen. Sooner or later one or the other is going to go, and Hank was ten years older. Perhaps if we had talked about it some more before he retired, we could have made another choice so I could have more money now. People should think twice, wives especially, about retirement benefits. It isn't so easy. You need that extra income.

Discussion

ANNA'S STORY IS SAD because it is like so many others I have heard. It doesn't have to be that way, either. Anna's reference to deducting money for her to receive after Hank was gone as part of his retirement pension is called "joint and survivor benefits."

Upon retirement, Hank was entitled to his *basic pension* from his company. This *basic pension* came from money the company put away for Hank's retirement.

When Hank retired years ago, his basic pension was $500 a month. Because he wanted to provide some income for Anna when he died, he looked into the different joint and survivor (J&S) options offered by his company. These options, or percentages, refer to how much of the original basic pension the surviving spouse will continue to receive. The higher the benefit percentage, the more the spouse will receive and the greater the deduction from the *basic pension* figure. Joint and survivor benefits usually are offered in the following percentages: 100 percent, 75 percent, 50 percent, and 25 percent. Most people opt to take the 50 percent option, as Hank did, thinking that when one partner dies, the other can get by with less money. Had he chosen the 100 percent joint and survivor benefit option, Anna would not be finding it so difficult to make ends meet. Let's look at Hank's figures more closely.

For the 50 percent joint and survivor benefit that Hank took, his basic pension was reduced by $15 a month, from receiving $500 to $485 a month for the rest of his life. That $15 a month would essentially act as a life insurance policy on Hank. When he died, though, Anna was entitled to only half of the $485, or $243 a month, because he chose the 50 percent option.

Selecting the 100 percent J&S option would have meant that the company would reduce his monthly pension of $500 to $450, or by $50 a month. That was $35 more a month than the 50 percent option. However, when Hank died, Anna would continue to receive 100 percent of Hank's pension, or $450 a month, for the rest of her life.

Hank mistakenly thought they needed more to live on while they were both around and Anna would not need nearly as much money to live on when he died. That is why he chose the 50 percent option. Besides, Hank thought Anna could always sell the house.

Even though pension amounts are significantly higher today than they were for Hank and Anna back in 1970, the concept is identical. Most people make the mistake of believing that their surviving spouse or partner does not, or will not, need as much money to live on as they both do now. *This is not the case in almost all situations.*

When you think about prices from twenty or thirty years ago, remember how much less things cost then and how much more it costs to live today? At the time of your retirement, most of you will still have another twenty to thirty years left to live. Don't make the same mistake of not thinking ahead, like Hank and Anna. If Hank did not believe they could make it on a reduction of $35 more a month for the 100 percent J&S benefit, then how could Anna make it twenty years later on a reduction of more than $240 a month from the pension alone?

When one partner dies, the surviving partner's expenses tend to increase, not decrease.

THE L(ONE)LINESS FACTOR

Being alone. While your partner is alive, you might be content to sit around on a Saturday night and watch TV and eat leftovers. But when one partner dies, to mask the loneliness, the desire to be with friends increases, and you might want to eat out more, see more movies, or go on more trips. Telephone calls and visits to other family members also increase.

Maintenance matters. On a more practical level, if the surviving partner is a woman, perhaps the male fixed the car or items around the house, which may have saved considerable money. For the first time Anna had to pay a mechanic to fix her car when it broke down. In fact, the upkeep, gasoline, insurance, registration, etc., became so expensive that Anna had to sell the car.

Taxes. Married couples, when filing jointly, may pay less in taxes. When a spouse dies, the tax bracket of the survivor changes. Anna went from filing jointly when Hank was alive to filing as a single. For example, the current tax for a $15,000-per-year income, for a couple filing jointly, is $600, compared to $1,455 for someone who files a singles return.

Losing one Social Security check. Another reason that Anna is in such financial trouble is that not only didn't they consider the effects of inflation, but also they did not consider that there would also be the loss of one Social Security check. Hank was receiving $600 a month in Social Security, and Anna received $300. When Hank died, Anna took over Hank's Social Security but lost hers. So not only was Hank's pension check to Anna reduced from $485 a month to $243, but also Anna lost another $300 from her Social Security check. The total reduction to Anna was $543 a month. Remember, with expenses that remain the same or increase, a reduction in pension and a loss of

TIP:

There are companies that allow joint and survivor benefits to unmarried and same-sex couples.

Social Security can change one's lifestyle dramatically.

Health insurance. Another element that can increase the expenses of the surviving spouse is health insurance costs. Upon the death of the worker, health insurance that the company may have paid for could suddenly become an added expense for the surviving partner. For instance, if Hank had died right after he retired and before both qualified for Medicare, Anna would have had to pay for her own health insurance.

Illness. When both partners are alive, one can care for the other during illness. After one partner dies, should the other become ill, temporary care can become an added expense.

Banking on the house. Like Hank, many men think their spouses can always sell the house. But Anna did not want to sell her house. She felt safe there and didn't have the slightest idea, after living in the same place for forty years, of how or where to begin to find another place to live. She also mentioned that if she sold the house, she would not know how to invest the money.

Don't put your partner in the precarious situation of selling the house just to pay the bills. What if the house doesn't sell right away? Besides, if your partner sells the house, he or she still has to live somewhere, and chances are that the least expensive place to live is the home you currently own.

THE INVOLVEMENT OF WOMEN

Statistics indicate that women outlive their husbands or male partners.* When Anna was asked if she was even aware that the choice Hank was making would impact on her life so much, her reply was, "No. Whatever Hank wanted was fine with me. He always said I would be okay, so I just didn't worry. I never thought it would end up this way. What bothers me the most is that if Hank had any idea of how I was living, he would be so upset. I know he thought he was doing the right thing for me."

Every *couple* must give serious thought to this decision together. When a woman's future depends on her partner's source of income, she must learn the facts and become involved in the final solution. The outcome will directly affect the surviving woman's quality of life. By taking charge and taking care of details now, old age can be rewarding and enjoyable.

When Anna was asked if she and Hank could have done without the $35 a month (the difference between the 100 percent option and the 50 percent option) for all those years, she said, "Oh, yes, we never really needed that money. Boy, do I wish I could turn back the hands of time."

Which joint and survivor benefit option you should take will be one of the most important decisions you will make regarding your retirement. Not all companies make it financially affordable to take a joint and survivor option. Each company has its own pricing structure, so you must first figure out how much each option will cost. The following will help guide you through this decision-making process if you are about to retire. If you are years away from retirement, your company may be able to do a projection so you can get an idea of what your joint and survivor benefits will be.

> **TIP:**
>
> *Most states require written permission from the spouse if anything below 50 percent benefit is taken.*

Guidelines

IS THE JOINT AND SURVIVOR BENEFIT OPTION THAT YOUR COMPANY IS OFFERING COST-EFFECTIVE?

Fill in the blanks from the information on your benefit sheet and follow the instructions on the next pages.

EXAMPLE A				
Item	J&S Options	Employee	Partner Benefit	Cost
1	Basic pension	(A)	(B)	(C)
2	50% option	(D)	(E)	(F)
3	100% option	(G)	(H)	(I)

Item 1:

- In (A) put the amount of your basic pension. This is how much the company will give you monthly. But, upon your death, your partner gets nothing.
- In (B) place a "0." This is how much your partner will receive from your pension benefits if you pass away first.
- In (C) place a "0." When you take this option, there is no cost to you because there is no survivor benefit to pay for. The company owes you the basic pension, and this is what it will pay you.

Item 2:

- In (D) put the dollar amount that appears in the "50 percent joint and survivor" section on your benefit statement.
- In (E) take (D) and divide by 2. This is what your partner will receive after your death. This figure should also appear on your benefit statement.
- In (F) subtract (D) from (A) and enter that sum here. This is the cost to you for the 50 percent option.

Item 3:

- In (G) place the dollar amount that appears in the "100 percent joint and survivor" section on your benefit statement.
- In (H) place the same figure that appears in (G). This is the benefit your surviving partner will receive. You should also find this figure on your benefit statement.
- In (I) subtract (G) from (A) and write this figure here. This is the cost to you for the 100 percent J&S option.

Once you have filled in the blanks, you will have something that looks like Example B. Let's examine the results of my clients Don and Janet. Don is fifty-six and his wife, Janet, is fifty-four. Don is about to take early retirement.

			EXAMPLE B		
Item	**J&S Options**	**Don**	**Janet**	**Cost**
1	Basic pension	$2,090 (A)	0 (B)	0 (C)
2	50% option	$2,000 (D)	$1,000 (E)	$ 90 (F)
3	100% option	$1,843 (G)	$1,843 (H)	$247 (I)

Explanation:

In Item 1, Don's basic pension is $2,090 a month. If they choose this option, Janet would receive absolutely nothing in monthly income upon Don's death. If they take the 50 percent joint and survivor benefit option in Item 2, the $2,090 is reduced to $2,000 for Janet to receive $1,000 a month upon Don's death. The cost to them for this option is $90 a month. In Item 3 the 100 percent J&S option reduces the $2,090 to

$1,843 a month to provide Janet with $1,843 a month for the rest of her life upon Don's death. The cost to them for this option is $247 a month.

Now that Don and Janet know what the cost to them will be for each J&S option, they need to decide which option they will take. Don and Janet decide that they want to take the 100 percent joint and survivor benefit of $1,843 per month. This will cost them $247 a month, or $2,964 a year. With that particular cost in mind, they want to know if there is another alternative outside the company that will be less costly and provide the same or better benefits for Janet. You see, selecting a joint and survivor benefit with the company could have some disadvantages.

DISADVANTAGES TO JOINT AND SURVIVOR BENEFITS FROM THE COMPANY

1. Essentially, what Don and Janet are doing by selecting a joint and survivor benefit option from the company is purchasing a so-called life insurance policy on Don through the company. The cost for this could be outrageous. Some companies or associations decrease the basic pension by more than half to provide a 100 percent J&S benefit. It may be more advantageous to purchase a policy outside the company. Is it possible for Don and Janet to purchase a life insurance policy on Don that would provide Janet with $1,843 a month upon Don's death for less than $247 a month?

2. Also, if Janet dies before Don, he is stuck paying $247 a month for the rest of his life for benefits no one else but Janet can use. Many companies are now offering what is called a *pop-up option* to protect against this. The pop-up option (each company may have its own name for this) allows Don to be reinstated to the basic pension amount if Janet predeceases him. More and more companies are utilizing this option for a small additional cost. Generally this *pop-up* option is limited to married couples, while the other J&S benefits are available to unmarried couples.

Even though there may be disadvantages, selecting a J&S option still has many advantages.

ADVANTAGES TO JOINT AND SURVIVOR BENEFITS FROM THE COMPANY

1. There are no health qualifications you must pass to receive these benefits.
2. It guarantees a monthly income for both partners for the rest of their lives.
3. There is nothing for you to do or worry about because you automatically get a check every month.

Even though there are advantages and disadvantages to the J&S options, each person's situation will be different. It is important to go through the exercise of comparing the following alternatives to your J&S benefits.

THE LIFE INSURANCE ALTERNATIVES

Don and Janet's alternatives to taking joint and survivor benefits with the company include the following:

1. They can purchase a *life* insurance policy on Don with the intention that when Don dies, Janet can invest the death proceeds and live off the interest generated. This interest would be equal to any J&S option they will choose.

or

2. Purchase a life insurance policy on Don and eventually purchase an annuity (see page 152 for definition) for Janet with the death proceeds. This will also provide monthly payments to Janet equal to any J&S option they choose.

or

3. A *term life* insurance policy can be purchased on Don coupled with an investment program to replace the term insurance completely when and if it expires. The main objective is to purchase an annuity for Janet when Don dies.

These alternatives could be especially pertinent for couples where there is a large difference in age. The larger the age difference, the greater the cost for the J&S benefit from the company. The reason for this is that the younger your partner, the longer the company will have to provide the benefit to that person.

In Don and Janet's case, we will explore the possibility of taking the full basic pension amount of $2,090 and purchasing life insurance on Don, and compare this to the 100 percent J&S benefit. When making these comparisons, keep this in mind:

If Don and Janet take the basic pension amount of $2,090 and do not select the J&S option with the idea in mind that they will purchase a life insurance policy, they will be taxed on all $2,090, with the result that there will be less than $247 left (the difference between the basic pension and the 100 percent J&S) to purchase a policy.

By taking the 100 percent J&S benefit from his company, the company simply reduces Don's basic pension by $247 a month. He will be taxed only on the amount he receives, or $1,843. The amount that goes to pay for Janet's benefit is essentially tax-free.

The life insurance alternatives are explored in order of preference.

ALTERNATIVE 1: BUYING A WHOLE-LIFE POLICY AND INVESTING THE DEATH PROCEEDS TO LIVE OFF THE INTEREST

The kind of policy you buy must offer the same security as the J&S benefits. If you live one year or a hundred years beyond your retirement, the policy must still be in effect so the surviving partner will have the death proceeds to invest to provide a monthly income equivalent to the J&S benefits.

The only type of policy that guarantees this is one that will cover you for your entire life, no matter how long that happens to be. Because this is guaranteed coverage, it can also be very expensive, so it is necessary to take the time and compare it to the cost of your J&S benefit payment. Insurance companies may refer to this type of policy by many different names. The most common among them is whole-life insurance. Regardless of what it is called, the only thing that matters is that the policy is guaranteed to pay a specific death benefit no matter how long you live and no matter what happens to interest rates.

The guarantees:

When shopping for an insurance policy, make sure to ask the agent for an illustration of the *guaranteed values of the policy*. These figures indicate the minimum amount the company will pay you regardless of what is happening with interest rates. Insurance companies publish these illustrations to protect the consumer, so you can see the worst- and best-case scenarios of what can happen to your money. When interest rates are high, insurance companies can offer lower premiums.

When rates are low, the insurance company has to adjust its rates accordingly. The result could be that it will cost you more in monthly premiums, or the company may lower the death benefit.

Whenever an illustration is given, you will see projected columns and guaranteed columns. The projected columns indicate what your policy will be worth if interest rates remain the same at the time of purchase. The guaranteed columns show what would happen in the worse-case scenario. It indicates the absolute minimum guaranteed amount the insurance company will give you. If the guaranteed columns fit your budget and future needs, then you know you can purchase the policy. If you are relying on the projected columns to meet your needs, you could be asking for trouble if interest rates do not continue to meet these expectations.

Don't let anyone tell you that the chance interest rates will decline to the minimum guaranteed level are remote. Policies I sold in 1984 that were originally paying 10 percent, 11 percent, or 12 percent in interest are currently paying only the absolute minimum guarantee of 4 percent (for those companies).

Advantages to buying a life insurance policy under this alternative:

1. Upon the death of the insured, a substantial sum of money will pass to the beneficiary tax-free. In a J&S option, upon the death of the worker, the survivor gets only a monthly taxable income.

2. If the insurance proceeds are invested in tax-free bonds or funds, the income generated is tax-free. Pension money is always fully taxable. An increase in tax brackets could make having an insurance policy a big plus.

3. Beside investing insurance proceeds in tax-free situations, they can also be invested to take advantage of interest rate changes. If rates move from 6 percent to 12 percent, this could dramatically change the income produced from the insurance proceeds and create a hedge against inflation. The company pension, on the other hand, most likely will not vary (unless they offer a cost-of-living increase).

4. If the spouse or partner dies first, the policy could simply be discontinued and the cash value of the policy withdrawn.

5. When the surviving spouse or partner dies, the entire proceeds can pass on to the beneficiaries.

The right amount of insurance to purchase:

Although the following will explain how to calculate how much insurance you will need, always check your figures with a professional advisor. Under this alternative your partner will have to live off the income from the proceeds of the life insurance policy until his or her death. Since we cannot predict that length of time, the safest way to protect your loved one is to make sure that the death proceeds received from the policy remain intact so there is enough to generate sufficient income for the surviving partner. The amount of insurance you will need to purchase will be directly affected by interest rates. The higher those rates, the less insurance is needed, and visa versa. Again, because these are unpredictable variables, using a moderate figure such as 5 percent is the best way to proceed. Even if interest rates are high when you first purchase the insurance, there is always the possibility that they could decline significantly at the time of death or afterward. Remember, when you take the J&S option with the company, the benefit amount is a set amount no matter what happens to interest rates.

Using the 5 percent assumed interest rate, follow the example to determine how much insurance Don and Janet should purchase. Take the amount Janet would receive from the J&S benefit, multiply by 12, and then multiply that total by 20.

The 100 percent J&S benefit amount that Janet would receive:

$$\begin{array}{r} \$\quad 1,843 \\ \times \qquad 12 \\ \hline = \$\quad 22,116 \\ \times \qquad 20 \\ \hline = \$442,320 \end{array}$$

Thus $442,320 is the amount of insurance Don and Janet will need to purchase, so when Don dies, Janet can invest the death proceeds at 5 percent to give her $1,843 a month in income.

To double-check the calculations, multiply the amount of life insurance by 5 percent and divide by 12 to get the monthly income amount.

$442,320 \times .05 = \$22,116 \div 12 = \$1,843$

Finding an insurance company:

As with any purchase you make, you want to deal with a reputable company that will endure. For this reason you should purchase a policy from a company that is rated by at least two of the five insurance rating companies and has the following desired rating. Call the rating services to check current ratings of companies you are interested in dealing with.

Name of Service	Desired Rating	Telephone Number
Standard & Poor's	AA or better	212-208-8000
A. M. Best	A+ +	908-439-2200
Moody's	Aa or better	212-553-0037
Duff & Phelps	Aa or better	312-263-2610
Weiss	B or better	407-627-3300*

*There will be a small charge to get ratings from this company.

Pricing a policy:

Now Don and Janet need to find out how much this insurance alternative will cost them. After they price a number of whole-life policies from different companies, they will compare those figures against the cost of the 100 percent J&S option. Can they purchase a $442,320 policy for $247 a month, which is what it will cost them if they take the 100 percent J&S option through the company?

Don and Janet compared and discovered it would cost them about $850 to $1,000 a month to purchase a $442,320 insurance policy. That's $600 to $800 more than taking the company's 100 percent J&S benefit option. So they decided to look into a second alternative.

ALTERNATIVE 2: PURCHASE A LIFE INSURANCE POLICY AND ANNUITY

Don and Janet can purchase a lesser amount of life insurance on Don wherein Janet can invest the death proceeds in an annuity that will provide $1,843 a month in income.

Buying a life insurance policy with the intention of purchasing an annuity to provide monthly income is the most comparable alternative to the J&S benefit; in both cases when the surviving partner dies, there is no lump sum payment to beneficiaries, and in many situations the monthly payments cease. If you intend to leave a large sum of money to your beneficiaries, you might reconsider the first alternative, but it will cost you more.

What is an annuity?

There are many types of annuities, but for our purposes we will consider the single-premium immediate annuity (SPIA). This type of annuity is a contract with an insurance company that guarantees to pay you a set amount of money every month for the rest of your life. After you give them a lump sum of money, the insurance company considers your life expectancy and the current interest rates, then calculates a figure they can pay you monthly. This monthly payment combines interest and a portion of your principal *and does not change*. Once you have handed over your money for an SPIA, you no longer have access to it other than your monthly stipend.

How much insurance should you purchase?

It is not as easy to figure out how much insurance is needed for this alternative because the amount of money needed to generate a specific payout every month will vary according to the person's age, as well as the current interest rate environments. The older you are when you purchase the annuity, and the higher the interest rates, the less money it will cost. The younger you are and the lower the interest rates, the higher the cost. In Don and Janet's case, since we can't know how old Janet will be when Don dies and what the interest rates will be, the amount of insurance to purchase is uncertain.

The best way for Don and Janet to reduce this uncertainty is to have an insurance agent or financial advisor do the calculations for them using the following assumptions:

1. Don dies immediately after retirement.
2. Interest rates are low. This means that the agent should use a very conservative interest rate factor when making this calculation.

In Don and Janet's case, using these assumptions, it is calculated that they will need to purchase $306,000 of insurance on Don. Should he die tomorrow, Janet would receive the entire amount to put into an annuity to get $1,843 a month for the rest of her life. Should Don die twenty years from now and rates are still low, Janet will need only $212,000 to generate that same $1,843 a month. With this in mind, it is also possible for Don and Janet to downsize their insurance policy as time goes on. Remember, the older you are when your partner dies, the less money you will need to put into an annuity.

How much will it cost Don and Janet to purchase $306,000 of life insurance? It is $700 a month. That is still $453 a month more than the 100 percent joint and survivor option with the company.

Are you beginning to think that joint and survivor benefits are the way to go? Well, there is a third alternative for Don and Janet to investigate.

ALTERNATIVE 3: TERM LIFE INSURANCE COUPLED WITH AN INVESTMENT PROGRAM

The third alternative for Don and Janet to investigate would be to purchase a term life insurance policy. It is considerably less expensive than a whole life policy but must eventually be replaced with savings or invested money to purchase an annuity.

Author's note: Although we are examining this alternative, I do not feel this is a viable option to replace a J&S benefit unless you fall under the category of special exceptions (see page 157). This option works best only for those people in their early fifties or younger. The reason I do not like this alternative is that very few people are disciplined enough to save on their own or know how to invest their money safely.

What is term life insurance?

Insurance that is good for a specific amount of time is referred to as "term" insurance. It may be good for one year, five years, ten years, or twenty, and is considerably less expensive than whole-life insurance. The insurance companies can afford to charge lower premiums because, statistically, you are not expected to die within the term of the policy. Therefore the chances the company will have to pay the death benefit are remote. When the term on the insurance runs out, the policy is repriced according to your age. The older you are, the greater the cost becomes. The cost of a term policy for someone in his or her seventies or eighties would be prohibitive. The insurance companies are in the business to protect their interests as well as yours, so it is highly unlikely that they will want to pay a beneficiary $400,000, for example, if they aren't absolutely sure they will be making at least this much in the long run. Term policies are wonderful to provide insurance for a short period of time, especially when you are younger and until you have time to build assets to replace the need for insurance.

Choosing the appropriate term:

Purchase a term policy for the longest period possible. Currently this is twenty years (referred to as a twenty-year level term policy, where the death benefits and premiums remain stable for all twenty years). We will see more about this later.

How much insurance should you buy?

To protect Janet, we will assume that Don will die the day after he retires. As we saw in Alternative 2, we need $306,000 from the death proceeds for Janet to purchase an annuity to provide her with $1,843 in monthly income. To figure out how much *you* need, be sure to have a financial advisor or insurance agent calculate this amount for you.

When Don and Janet researched the cost of a twenty-year level term policy, they discovered it would cost them only $250 a month. This seemed appealing until I informed them that they needed an investment program to accompany the insurance to be able to re-place it when it expired in twenty years.

The investment program:

Since we know that the term policy will most likely expire before Don dies, and the older Don gets the more expensive it will be to renew, they must begin to build assets to replace the term policy when it expires. Since the amount of money needed will be substantial, it will take a long time to accumulate. This is why you should purchase a term policy for the longest period possible. How much do Don and Janet need to save in twenty years to replace the policy? Again, this is a cal-culation you should do with a professional advisor.

As we have seen in Alternative 2, Janet will need only $212,000 to purchase an annuity if Don dies the day after the policy expires (Janet will be seventy-four at that time). To save $212,000 over the next twenty years, Don and Janet will have to put away $522 a month, assuming a 5 percent interest rate. This, along with the premiums for the term insurance of $250 a month, brings their total monthly cost to $772. This is still $525 more a month than simply opting for the 100 percent J&S benefit with the company. Can you guess which choice Don and Janet made?

You may find that due to the pricing structure your company is using, or the age and/or health difference between you and your partner, buying a life insurance policy may really be an option. Even though it was not for Don and Janet, it behooves you to go through these exercises to see if a life insurance policy in your particular situation could be a better choice. Be sure to have a good life insurance agent or financial advisor help you with the calculations. For most of you, however, the 100 percent J&S benefit will best suit your needs.

If it is decided that life insurance is a good alternative for you, then the question of when to purchase insurance must be addressed.

WHEN TO PURCHASE INSURANCE

Replacing the J&S benefit with a life insurance policy requires not only that you apply for the policy before retirement, but that you are accepted and everything is in place as well. Here is a story of what could happen:

Before Joe retired, he compared the cost of the J&S options with the life insurance alternatives. Because Joe was significantly older than his wife, Katie, the insurance alternative was more cost-effective. So he took his basic pension when he retired. Shortly after retirement, Joe filled out a life insurance application and had the routine medical examination. Much to his surprise and dismay, a dark spot was discovered on his lung X ray. It turned out to be cancer. Joe's life insurance application was turned down, leaving Katie with no income should he die.

Joint and survivor benefit options are automatic. There are no health requirements. If Joe had only applied for his insurance before retirement, he would have had the option to take the J&S plan to protect Katie, even though he was seriously ill at the time. *If you have opted for the life insurance alternative, you must apply and be accepted before you retire.*

One final note: With all the possible alternatives presented, most of you will find that the joint and survivor benefit through your company will be the most cost-effective and beneficial option.

If a financial advisor indicates that you should take anything less than the 100 percent joint and survivor option, *I am firmly countering this advice.* Unless you are guaranteed to receive a significant inheritance or windfall within the very near future, have considerable liquid assets, or if insurance is an option, the 100 percent J&S option is highly recommended, *with these special exceptions:*

1. When your nonworking partner is much older than you;
2. When the nonworking partner has a serious or terminal illness.

A word of caution: When either of the two exceptions is the case, people tend to take the basic pension (where the partner will receive nothing), thinking the nonworking partner will most assuredly die first. On the surface this seems logical, but it can work to your detriment, as you see below.

Leon's wife, Ruth, was diagnosed with terminal cancer. Leon retired from his job to spend more time with her. When his company presented the joint and survivor benefits, Leon figured it would cost him $300 a month to provide Ruth with the 100 percent option and $175 a month for the 50 percent option. The company did not offer the "pop-up" option, so Leon and

Ruth decided not to take any of these options, since she was expected to die within several months. Ruth also wanted Leon to have as much as possible to live on once she was gone. They took the basic pension. Two months after Leon retired, he was killed in an automobile accident. Ruth lived another eighteen months, with no income.

We can never know how things are going to turn out. It is important that we always take the proper precautions, just in case.

HOW TO PROTECT THE ONES YOU LOVE AS WELL AS YOURSELF

POP-UP OPTION

If your company offers the *pop-up* option, that will be very useful under these circumstances. Let's say Leon and Ruth had taken the 100 percent "pop-up" joint and survivor benefit. If Ruth had died first, as originally anticipated, Leon would then return to his basic pension amount. He would not have to continue paying for a benefit that no one would use. On the other hand, when Leon was killed in the car crash, Ruth would have continued to receive all of Leon's pension. With the pop-up option both Leon and Ruth were protected.

NO POP-UP OPTION

If your company does not offer this option, as was the case with Ruth and Leon, term life insurance could be the answer.

Depending on age you may purchase term life insurance fairly inexpensively. It's perfect for a situation where you know you will need insurance for only a few years at most. In the case where Leon died before Ruth, term life insurance would have ensured that she would be cared for financially. Another benefit to having term life insurance on Leon in this type of situation is that when Ruth dies, there could be a sizable sum to leave to their children from the insurance proceeds.

Everyone's situation will be different and we cannot predict the future, but we can try to protect it.

THE 100 PERCENT J&S OPTION AS AN INVESTMENT

Many of you may now be convinced to take the 100 percent J&S option offered by the company. Others may still believe they need only take the 50 percent option to protect their partner. Besides urging you to reread the Discussion section of this chapter to change your mind, the 100 percent option over the 50 percent option may be the best financial investment you could make. Here's why:

Don's basic pension is $2,090. Even though he is reasonably sure, with their other assets, that his wife, Janet, will need only the 50 percent option to pay all the bills, he has decided to see if it makes economic sense to take the 100 percent option over 50 percent option. The 50 percent J&S option will reduce his basic pension by $90 a month to $2,000, but Janet will receive only $1,000 a month when he dies. If he takes the 100 percent option, his monthly pension will be reduced by $247 a month, to $1,843. This is also how much Janet will continue to receive.

The difference to Don's pension check between the two options is $157 a month ($2,000 minus $1,843). The difference to Janet when Don dies will be $843 a month ($1,843 minus $1,000). Don wanted to know if it was worth paying the extra $157 a month now to give Janet $843 more a month later. Here is how he would figure it out:

Don is only fifty-six years old and has a life expectancy of about twenty-seven more years. So he would take the $157 and multiply it by 12 to find out how much more it will cost per year to select the 100 percent option over the 50 percent option.

$$\$157 \times 12 = \$1,884$$

Multiply his life expectancy of twenty-seven years by the yearly cost:

$$\$1884 \times 27 = \$50,868 \text{ total cost}$$

Over Don's life expectancy of twenty-seven years, he will spend a total of $50,868 for the 100 percent option over the 50 percent option. That seems like a lot of money to spend. Is it worth it?

If Don chooses the 100 percent option, Janet will receive $843 more each month, or $10,116 per year.

$$\$843 \times 12 = \$10,116 \text{ additional yearly income}$$

Given these figures, how much longer will Janet have to live beyond Don to recoup all $50,688? Divide the total expected cost by the additional income:

$$\$50,688 \div \$10,116 = 5.01 \text{ years}$$

Janet will have to live only five years more than Don to get the total cost back.

Let's go one step farther. For every year Janet lives beyond those 5 years, she will be making a 20 percent per year return on that money. How did we get this figure? Divide the additional yearly income by the total cost:

$$\$10,116 \div \$50,688 = 20\%$$

Don realizes that the chances of Janet living at least five years longer than he are good, especially since women statistically outlive men. Besides, there are very few places that one can get a 20 percent return on funds. So Don and Janet decided to take the 100 percent joint and survivor option, even though they expected that Janet will not need the money. If Don dies before his full life expectancy, the return will be even greater.

If you are in a situation where you know that your partner will definitely not need the money, then you should consider this option strictly from an investment position.

Everyone should take the time to figure their particular investment return. The results will depend on your age, the age of your partner, the amount of your basic pension, the cost of the joint and survivor benefit, etc. Use the following calculations as a guide.

If you are in good health, assume a life expectancy to age eighty-three.

1. Subtract your current age from 83:
   83 − _____ = _____(a) age difference

2. Subtract the 50 percent option payment from the 100 percent option payment. Refer to your figures in boxes (D) and (G) in Example A, page 123.
   (G) − (D) = _____(b) difference

3. Multiply (b) by 12 to get the annual cost:
   (b) × 12 = _____(c) annual cost

4. Multiply (c), annual cost, by (a), age difference, to get the total cost over your expected life:
   (c) × (a) = _____(d) total cost

5. From Example A, subtract (E) from (H) to give you the difference in total monthly income for the surviving spouse:
   H − E = _____(e) difference in total monthly income

6. Multiply (e), difference in total monthly income, by 12 to get the annual figure (f).
   (e) × 12 = _____(f) annual figure

7. Divide (d), total cost, by (f), difference in total yearly income, to find out how many years it will take to recoup that investment:

$$(d) \div (f) = \underline{\hspace{1cm}}(g) \text{ years}$$

8. To find out how much you will make on your investment for every year that you live beyond (g), divide (f) by (d):

$$(f) \div (d) = \underline{\hspace{1cm}}\text{annual return on investment}$$

When deciding the financial future of someone you love, you must take the time to consider your objectives and their ramifications. Once a joint and survivor option has been chosen, it is irreversible. All too often people think they should have more money to live on now and don't consider the future consequences, like Hank and Anna. One question that I am always asked when I cover this topic in my retirement seminars is, "Why can't I simply take my basic pension and invest some of it on my own to accumulate what is needed twenty or thirty years from now to provide a survivor's income? Isn't that essentially what the company is doing with my money?" If we could forecast the day when we are going to die, this would be an option. Since we don't know when this will happen, we might not have the years needed to accumulate the necessary amount. You cannot afford to tempt fate.

Minimize Your Expenses/ Maximize Your Income

For most of us, the main reason we cannot afford to retire or make ends meet is simply that our expenses are greater than our income. It really doesn't matter how it happened; what counts is what we can do to make our financial lives work better.

This chapter is filled with advice I have given my clients to help them retire more comfortably. We will look at your debts, reorganize them, get rid of as many as possible, and count the dollars as they add up.

The Goal of Retirement

WHEN LESS IS MORE!

Ultimately, the goal of retirement is to become as debt-free as possible. For most of us, though, the first step will be to make sure the debts that we do have are intelligent ones. It does not make any sense to owe $3,000 on your credit cards at an interest rate of 18 percent that is not tax-deductible when you have $3,000 sitting in a money market fund earning 2 percent. You are losing money! Many people fear spending their available cash and would rather remain in debt while losing interest every year on their money, in this case 16 percent.

To turn the tide of our debts, we must look at the following three things:

1. current debt: how much you owe and how much it is costing you (interest charged);
2. total assets: how much you have and how much it is making for you (interest earned);
3. reorganizing those debts.

YOUR DEBTS

List all debts (*excluding* home mortgages) *in order of interest rates*—from highest to lowest. Add anything else you can think of. For example, you owe Visa $3,000 at an interest rate of 18 percent. You also owe MasterCard $5,000 but the interest rate is 15 percent. List the Visa first. Use this list as your guide:

Debt Name	Interest Rate	X Total Owed	Y Payment per Month	No. of Years Left
Visa				
MasterCard				
Discover Card				
Credit union				
Auto				
Dept. stores				
Personal loans				
Student loans				
Other				
Total				

Place the following figures here:
Total debt amount (column X) $ _____ (X)
Total monthly payments (column Y) $ _____ (Y)

Before your debts can be reorganized and minimized, a clear picture of all your assets is needed. This will take a little extra work on your part.

YOUR LIQUID ASSETS

In Table A list all your liquid assets. This is money, not investments, that you can access in a matter of days without penalties or taxes.

TABLE A	
Asset	**Amount**
Savings accounts	
Money market funds	
Checking accounts	
Credit unions	
Safe deposit box	
Other	
	Total $ _____ (A)

In Table B list any money needed or already targeted for a major expense in the future.

TABLE B	
Expense	**Amount**
Auto purchase	
Home down payment	
Home repair	
Auto repair	
Vacation	
Child's marriage	
Education	
Motor home purchase	
Boat	
Real estate	
Plastic surgery	
Other	
	Total $ _____ (B)

Subtract (B) from (A) to get an actual cash figure (C) available to reduce debts.

TABLE C		
Total cash	$ _____	(A)
Total money needed	$ _____	(B)
Total available to reduce debts	$ _____	(C)

If there is no cash at all, that is okay. Skip to the section "Your Home—Your New Best Friend!" If you do not have a home, skip to the section "When You Don't Know What Else to Do, Try This!"

In Table D list all your assets invested for growth that can be liquidated within a few days. Also list the annual return you are getting on each of these investments.

TABLE D		
Type of Investment	**Amount**	**Annual Return**
Stocks		
Mutual funds		
Certificates of deposit		
Treasury bills		
Treasury notes		
Treasury bonds		
Corporate bonds		
Municipal bonds		
Other		
Total that could be liquidated $ _____ (D)		

REAL ESTATE

List any real estate you own in Table E.

TABLE E

Your personal residence
(home):
   Current value $ _____
   Minus amount owed on first   − $ _____
mortgage
     Subtotal   = $ _____
   Minus any outstanding   − $ _____
equity loans
Total equity available in home   = $ _____(E)

   Additional information:

Interest rate on mortgage   _____%
Is your mortgage fixed or   _____
variable?
Number of years left on   _____
mortgage
Monthly payment $ _____
Interest rate on equity loan   _____%
Monthly payment $ _____
Number of years left on loan   _____

   Other real estate owned:

Current value $ _____
Minus amount owed on first   − $ _____
mortgage
   Subtotal   = $ _____
Minus any outstanding equity   − $ _____
loans
Total equity available   = $ _____

   Additional information:

Interest rate on mortgage   _____%
Is your mortgage fixed or   _____
variable?
Number of years left on   _____
mortgage
Monthly payment $ _____
Interest rate on equity loan   _____%
Monthly payment $ _____
Number of years left on loan   _____

Repeat these questions for each property owned.

MINIMIZING YOUR CURRENT AND FUTURE DEBT

To help make better use of your money, you must now determine whether any debts can be reduced or re-organized, using the following options.

USING CASH TO PAY DOWN YOUR DEBTS

Enough cash: Look at your total amount of debt (X) and compare that with line (C), your available cash to reduce debts. If (C) exceeds your debt, consider paying off these debts with this cash. The only time it makes sense to have *any* debt is when you are earning more on your cash than you are paying on your debts. Since this is most likely not the case, *it will be best, in the long run, to pay off all your debts with the available cash.*

Some cash: If you do not have as much cash as is needed to pay off all your debts, take as much as you feel comfortable with and pay off whatever debts you can. Be sure to *pay off those debts with the highest interest rates first.*

No cash: If you don't have any cash to pay off the debts, the next step is to look at your investments, as indicated in Table D.

If you do not have any investments, skip to the section "Your Home—Your New Best Friend!"

INVESTMENTS

Are your investments earning as much as you are paying on your debts? For instance, if you are paying 19 percent on your credit cards, are your investments earning that much? Probably not. The quickest way to guarantee a 19 percent return on your money is to liquidate your investments and pay off your high-interest debt.

CAUTION: DO NOT DO THIS BEFORE CONSULTING A TAX ADVISOR AND FINANCIAL ADVISOR. THE TAX CONSEQUENCES OF DOING THIS MAY WIPE OUT ANY ADVANTAGES.

PAY YOURSELF BACK—REPLACE THOSE ASSETS

If you have eliminated your debt with your assets, it is very important to replace those assets. Continue to pay yourself monthly as though you are paying off the debts.

Kimi was paying $500 a month to various credit card companies. She decided to take $7,000 from an account and pay off the entire amount she owed. She continued to put $500 a month, the amount she had been paying to credit card companies, into her savings account. In fourteen months she had her $7,000 back and no debts.

Even if you do not pay yourself as much as you were sending your creditors, set aside whatever you can on a monthly basis. Before you know it, you will have replaced those funds you used to pay off your debt and established a disciplined saving habit.

YOUR HOME—YOUR NEW BEST FRIEND

In most cases, your principal residence can be used to reduce the amount of those high monthly payments and offer you the security that your cash on hand gives you. There are three main ways to use your home to help you become as debt-free as possible:

1. Refinance your home.
2. Take out a home equity loan.
3. Pay off your home.

Compare the interest rate you are paying on your home to that of your other debts. Most likely your home will have the lowest interest rate. Your principal residence usually qualifies for the best interest rate a consumer can get. Not only are they low, but they are also tax-deductible. With this in mind, it may be advantageous to use the equity in your home to reduce other interest expenses. Your particular circumstances will determine whether to refinance or to take out a home equity loan.

REFINANCING

Refinancing is simply replacing (refinancing) the current mortgage on your home with another mortgage from a bank or financial institution. People refinance when mortgage interest rates are lower than their current mortgage rate.

Refinancing makes sense only when *all* of the following apply:

- You plan to keep your home for at least the next few years.
- You have at least nine to ten years left on your current mortgage.
- Current interest rates are at least 1 to 2 percentage points lower than your present mortgage.

Reasons to refinance:
- To decrease payments on the mortgage alone and/or combine other current debts into the mortgage.
- You have a variable loan, where the mortgage payments change with fluctuating interest rates, and

you want to change to a fixed-rate mortgage, where payments remain stable over the life of the loan. This is especially desirous if interest rates are currently low and it looks as if they are starting to go back up.

TIP:

Refinancing makes sense only if you are going to stay in the house longer than it takes to recoup your closing costs.

Refinancing simply to lower your debt interest rate when you cannot lower your mortgage rate as well is not the most efficient way to rid yourself of high-interest debts. Those costs to refinance a loan known as closing costs could be several thousand dollars. If your goal is simply to lower the payments on your outstanding debt (aside from your mortgage), you would be better off with a home equity loan (see page 175). If, on the other hand, you are able to lower the interest rate on your mortgage as well as on your outstanding debts, refinancing becomes desirable.

Wanda's situation was ideal for refinancing. Wanda's home is valued at $185,000. She still owes $95,000 at an interest rate of 8 percent. Over the years she has run up $29,000 in debts, with an average interest rate of 15 percent. Her monthly payments on her debts total $1,000. Wanda's dilemma is that she has been offered early retirement and she wants to take it. We did all the necessary calculations (see page 118) to see if she could afford to retire early, but she came up short $500 a month.

Since interest rates were at 6.5 percent, I had Wanda refinance her home for $124,000—the $95,000 for her original mortgage loan plus the $29,000 she owed in credit card debts. Her payments on the new mortgage increased only $181 a month, even with the added $29,000. Still, that is $819 less a month than she was paying to the credit card companies.

Since Wanda needed only $500 more a month to take the early retirement offer, she could now do so and put away $319 a month to build up her cash reserve. Wanda also benefited because she converted a

TIP:

1. Try to find a mortgage that has the least expensive closing costs. If a loan has a good interest rate but will cost you "an arm and a leg" to get it, it is not to your benefit. Always figure out how long it will take to recoup your closing costs.

2. If you do not plan to sell your home within the next few years and if it will take you more than three years to get back your closing costs, look for another loan with more reasonable costs.

non-tax-deductible debt to a tax-deductible one, further increasing her savings.

Here's how to make sure it pays to refinance:

Take your current mortgage payment $ _____

Subtract what your mortgage payment
will be if you refinance $ _____
Equals your monthly savings $ _____ (A)
Take the total closing costs
to refinance $ _____ (B)
Divide your closing cost (B) by monthly savings (A)
Equals number of months to recoup closing costs
     _____ months
To get the number of years it will take you
to recoup the money you paid in closing costs,
divide the number of months by 12
     = _____ years

Melissa and Lynn own a home together. Their current interest rate is 8.5 percent. They could refinance at 6.5 percent. The only hitch is that they know they will be selling their house in the next two years to move to New Mexico. The question is: Even though the monthly payments will be lower, will it really save money in the long run? Should they refinance? The total closing costs to refinance would be $3,600.

The amount of the new loan is	$120,000
Take the current mortgage payment	$1,181
Subtract the refinanced payment	−$1,045
Equals your monthly savings	$ 136
Total closing costs	$ 3,600
Divide by monthly savings	÷ $136
Equals number of months to recoup closing costs	26.5 months
Divide by 12 for number of years	= 2.2 years

So it will take Melissa and Lynn 2.2 years to recoup the amount they paid in closing costs. That is longer than they plan to keep the house. It is not worthwhile for them to refinance, at least with this particular mortgage lender.

Refinancing and taxes:

For tax purposes, don't overlook this deduction. If you have refinanced your home mortgage in the recent past and refinanced again because interest rates went down even further, those points you may have paid to the lender the previous time are now tax-deductible in one lump sum. For example: You refinanced your home a few years ago and paid $3,600 in points. These points can only be deducted off your taxes by spreading the amount over the life of the loan. So the $3,600 on a fifteen-year loan allowed you to deduct only $240 a year on your taxes. Now that you refinanced again, the remaining balance on the points you paid on the previous loan are now tax-deductible in their entirety. In other words, you deducted $240 for two years, or $480 of the $3,600, and by refinancing again, you now get to deduct the balance of $3,120 on your income-tax return.

DON'T WASTE THE PAST:

When refinancing, take into consideration that you are adding years back onto your loan.

Sam has a fifteen-year mortgage at 8.85 percent. The original mortgage amount was $150,000, and his monthly payments are $1,508. Sam has been paying the loan for the past six years and has only nine years left and a balance of $110,000. If he refinanced a new fifteen-year loan at 7 percent, his monthly payments will be $989, but he will be adding six years to the life of the loan. The total cost to him over the next fifteen years, until the house is paid off, would be $178,020 ($989 × 180 months). If he did not refinance and

TIP:

Look at the whole picture. Monthly savings aren't necessarily the best reason to refinance if you do not save money in the long run.

simply continued paying $1,508 a month, since he has only 9 years left on his current loan, it would cost him a total of $162,864 ($1,508 × 108). Even though his monthly payments would be less, the loan would end up costing him $15,156 more, plus closing costs of $2,500, for a total of $17,656.

I had Sam refinance his home to take advantage of the lower interest rate, but I increased his monthly payments to $1,376 a month rather than the required $989, so he could pay off his house loan in nine years. This is still $132 less each month than the $1,508 he was paying. Over the next nine years he will save $14,256. Even if closing costs are $2,500, it would be worthwhile.

GETTING BY

For many of you, however, it may not be a question of what saves you more in the long run, but a question of how to get by now! Converting credit card debts or other high-interest-rate debts to a home mortgage could reduce the monthly burden. However, the reason you pay less is not due to the lower interest rate, but that you are paying the debt over a longer period of time. Generally, the longer you pay, the more you pay overall.

For the lowest monthly payments, look into a thirty-year loan rather than a fifteen-year loan. Even though this is more costly in the long run, it may be best if you need to get by now. Certainly when things start to pick up for you, there is always the option of paying off your mortgage earlier. Never get a loan with a prepayment, or early payoff, penalty. Check the difference between the fifteen- and thirty-year loan rates. If they are essentially the same, get the fifteen-year loan. If you are only looking for a way to decrease your monthly payments on your high-interest debts, consider looking into a home equity loan.

HOME EQUITY LOANS

A home equity loan is an extended line of credit, up to a certain amount, given by a financial institution against the accrued additional value, or the equity, in your home (the current value minus what you owe). It is when you actually use these funds that you begin to pay for the loan. So merely having a home equity loan or line of credit does not cost you anything. Using it will.

Interest rates on home equity loans fluctuate the same as those for variable-rate home loans, but home equity loans do not have the high closing costs that refinancing does. The only cost associated with a home equity loan should be the appraisal of your home to verify the value and equity.

To qualify for a home equity loan you must have sufficient income and equity in your home—see page 167, line (E). For the most part, home equity loans are tax-deductible.

Home equity loans make sense only when any of the following apply:

- You need money for a short period of time— a few years at most.
- You will be selling your home within two years and need some extra cash.
- Interest rates are projected to go lower.
- You need a source of funds in case of an emergency.
- You want to lower the interest rates on your debts but not on your mortgage.

Best ways to use a home equity loan:

Cash replacement. Are you one of those people who is afraid to use your cash for fear that something might happen and you will need it? Having an equity loan is great for just such emergencies and debt payments.

Nancy owed $9,000 in credit card debts. She kept about $10,000 sitting in her checking account for emergencies. Like so many others, she was afraid to use all her available cash to pay off her credit cards. She felt better continuing to pay 18 percent on her credit cards while earning a mere 2 percent on her cash, just to know the cash is there if she ever needs it.

Creating "intelligent" debt. Nancy does own a home that has a considerable amount of equity. She applied for a home equity loan and qualified for a loan of up to $50,000. Because Nancy is a spender and she knows it, she told the bank that she wanted a line of credit for only $10,000. She certainly didn't want to go further into debt through temptation. Isn't that how we all get into debt in the first place?

Nancy can now take her funds out of the bank and pay all her credit card debts. She need not fret because she knows if she needs money, all she has to do is write a check from her equity line of credit. If she does use the credit line, it will most assuredly be at a lower rate of interest and be tax-deductible.

Now that she no longer has credit card payments, every month she writes a check to herself instead of the credit card company. As long as she is able to, she puts the money back into her account. In "no time at all" she will have saved the $9,000 again.

BEFORE YOU PAY OFF ANY DEBT

• Before using all your cash to pay off any debt, first apply and qualify for the equity loan. Be sure to shop around, since equity loans vary from one financial institution to another. Often, when there is a great deal of equity in the property, the financial institution will offer you a substantial line of credit. Even if you qualify for such a large amount, as Nancy did, have the bank issue you a line of credit equal only to the amount you will need to pay off your debts. Remember, you are doing this to get out of debt, not create more.

• Second, after you qualify, take the money you have in your account and pay all your debts. Fear is no longer a factor now that you have your equity line of credit.

• Third, continue paying the same monthly payments from your credit card debt back into your account to replenish the funds you took out.

If you do not have enough in your accounts to pay all the debts, or none at all, a home equity loan can still be very useful. When the interest rates on your debts are higher than the home equity loan rates, transfer the debt from the credit card companies to the home equity loan line.

BRIDGING THE GAP

Many may not have any ready cash on hand (that's most of us), but maybe we have investments, such as CDs, that will be maturing in a year or two. Because taking out those funds prior to maturity will be penalized, an equity line of credit can be used to pay off the higher-interest-rate debts. When these investments mature, the equity loan can be paid back with the funds from those investments. *Remember, the goal is to be debt-free!*

THE LOW-INTEREST-RATE ENVIRONMENT

Because the interest rates of a home equity loan fluctuate, it is not recommended to use an equity line of credit if you need money for a long time. Refinancing when interest rates are low will be more appropriate, especially if you can get a fixed rate with low closing costs. Remember, refinancing makes sense only if you do not plan to sell in the next few years. If you do plan to sell, it would be better to use a home equity loan.

THE HIGH-INTEREST-RATE ENVIRONMENT

If interest rates are high and are projected to come down, a home equity line of credit is more advantageous than refinancing. Since home equity loans generally do not have closing costs, you really have nothing to lose. Interest rates on most home equity loans are variable. Should interest rates start to come down, you will benefit. When interest rates come down considerably, that will be the time to refinance and switch to a fixed loan if you plan to keep the house for a number of years.

HOUSE FOR SALE

If you know you will be selling your house in the next few years and you have other high-interest-rate debts, a home equity loan could be the answer. After you sell your home, you can pay off the line of credit.

PAYING OFF THE MORTGAGE

For a few of you, another way to decrease your monthly expenses is by paying off the mortgage on your home.

When is this a good idea? When your current investments are not consistently earning as high a return as you are paying on your mortgage *and* you have more than five years left to pay on your mortgage.

My Mom owed $20,000 on her condo. She was paying 10 percent interest on her mortgage and had ten years left to pay on it. Like a lot of people, she had $20,000 stashed in her savings account, making 2 percent. She is not in a high tax bracket, so the tax deduction she received for the mortgage payment did not really benefit her.

I asked her if she would like a "no risk" investment that would guarantee 10 percent on her money. Without hesitation, she replied enthusiastically, "Yes, of course." At that point I advised her to take the cash and pay off her mortgage.

Though she was miffed at my approach with her, she paid off her mortgage in full and decreased her monthly expenses by more than $200. She now feels secure knowing her home is paid in full, and she pays herself with that $200 a month.

WHEN YOU DON'T KNOW WHAT ELSE TO DO, TRY THIS!

You may be in a situation where none of these suggestions can help you, whether it is because you don't have any cash or investments, find refinancing or a home equity loan an impossible option due to bad credit or devaluation of the property, or you don't own a home.

If you cannot meet your monthly bills and you really don't know what to do, here are my suggestions:

Ask a friend or a relative to help. They may be willing to loan you the money to pay your debts at a better interest rate than what you are currently paying. You can arrange to pay that person monthly rather than the companies you are now paying.

Don't be afraid to ask. You may also be doing them a favor. Perhaps they are in a fixed-income situation where they need as much income on investments as possible. You can offer them a higher interest rate than they can get elsewhere and still get a lower rate for yourself.

Remember, everything you do must be done with integrity. If you are really getting far behind on your payments and you are dodging the calls from your creditors, it's time to face them before things get out of hand. Call and tell them that you are in a financial bind and can afford to send only $ _____ (you fill in the blank) a month. Most creditors, including the IRS, will be happy to strike a deal to get something rather than nothing at all. Once you have made that agreement with them, you should stick to it. If you cannot, call them back again and tell them. It may be a tedious process, but it will accomplish what you have set out to do.

When refinancing your home is not an option to help reduce monthly mortgage payments, you can call your mortgage company and see if they will offer a "hardship case" reduction of interest. It is to their benefit to do this, since they will be just as hard-pressed to sell a devalued house as you would be. This only works, however, if the interest rate you are paying is higher than current interest rates.

REVERSE MORTGAGES

There is another way in which your home may be able to serve you later in life.

As we retire and get older, we tend to cling to the surroundings that are familiar to us—our home, the street and neighbors, and the local shops. More often than not, our home is really the only asset we have, especially if it is paid for. If this is the case and you get in a situation where you need some extra cash, perhaps you can access the equity in your home with what is known as a reverse mortgage.

Simply put, instead of paying the bank, the bank pays you. With a reverse mortgage, you receive a monthly amount of money based on equity, your age, current interest rates, and how long you want them to pay you. You can live in the house as long as you want. You can even sell the house and pay back the bank. Upon your death, when the house passes to your heirs, they can either pay the loan with other funds or sell the house to pay the bank what you owe them.

QUALIFYING FOR A REVERSE MORTGAGE

For some, when extra income is needed, a reverse mortgage is much easier to acquire than refinancing. When you refinance, you must pay the bank every month for the money you have taken for additional income, so you are responsible to invest that money to generate enough income to live on as well as pay the bank. If you fail to pay the bank or miss monthly payments, the bank will begin foreclosure proceedings, and you could lose the house. With a regular mortgage you also have to qualify and meet certain income requirements, which may not be possible if you are already in need.

When applying for a reverse mortgage, income is not taken into consideration, so it is easier to qualify. To qualify, all that is required is that:

- you own your home and live in it;
- you have maintained it in good condition;
- you are sixty years of age or older.

There is no chance of losing your home because the bank pays you; you do not pay the bank.

TYPES OF REVERSE MORTGAGES

Reverse mortgages vary, but there are three basic types to choose from:

Tenure reverse mortgage can provide you with a stream of payments for the rest of your life or until you leave your home.

Term reverse mortgage only provides you with income for a specified term or number of years. When the term is up, so are your payments. This particular type of reverse mortgage tends to give you higher monthly payments because they are for a shorter time.

Line of credit reverse mortgage works like a home equity loan. The bank gives you a checkbook with a line of credit for a certain amount. Every time you need money, you just write yourself a check. The difference is, with a regular equity loan, you must make monthly payments; with a reverse mortgage, you make no payments, and the money is paid back when the house is sold or by your beneficiaries.

FHA REVERSE MORTGAGES

There are currently more than 10,000 institutions that are guaranteed by the FHA (Federal Housing Administration) to offer a reverse mortgage. Reverse mortgages are backed by the FHA guarantee stating that you or your estate will never owe more than the house is worth. For instance, if you took out a tenure reverse mortgage, the bank pays you an income for the rest of your life. It is quite possible, depending on how long you live, that the bank will have paid you more than the house is worth. When the house is eventually sold, they will not make as much as they gave and will have lost money. The FHA guarantee states that if this happens, the bank cannot come back to your estate to get that extra money. An FHA-insured reverse mortgage guarantees payment to homeowners even if the lender goes out of business. Because these guarantees are there to protect you, stick with a reverse mortgage offered by an FHA institution.

Before doing anything, though, research reverse mortgages carefully. As an applicant interested in reverse mortgages, you may be required to learn more about them through your local office on aging. As reverse mortgages become increasingly popular, many other lenders will be entering the arena by offering new variations, such as linking the reverse mortgage to annuities to allow you to continue to receive income even after you sell your home. When the National Federal Mortgage Association (Fannie Mae) introduces its own reverse mortgage program, there will be an increasing availability of such loans.

For more information and a monthly updated list of institutions offering reverse mortgages, send $1 and a self-addressed, stamped envelope to:

The Reverse Mortgage Locator
National Center for Home Equity Conversion
7373 147th Street West, Suite 115
Apple Valley, MN 55124
Tel: 612-953-4474

Don't think of your home just as something you live in; also think of it as something that can help you when you need money to live on!

The AARP (American Association of Retired Persons) also has a guide to reverse mortgages called *Home Made Money*. It is free by writing to:

Publication D12894
AARP Fulfillment (EE0597)
601 E Street, NW
Washington, D.C. 20049
Tel: 800-424-3410

Another free brochure, called "Facts for Consumers—Reverse Mortgages," can be obtained by writing to:

Federal Trade Commission
Public Reference Branch
Sixth Street and Pennsylvania Avenue, NW
Washington, D.C. 20580
Tel: 202-326-2222

A reverse mortgage is an idea to keep in mind if you ever need to maximize your income.

RENTAL PROPERTY

Do you own rental property or a second home you are still financing? The mortgage rates on these properties will generally be higher than for your primary residence. If you have enough equity in your home, refinance your home, and use the cash to pay off the other properties. The debts have been consolidated into one at a lower interest rate.

BANKING

Search for a bank that does not charge for account services. Some banks have special reduced rates or no fees for senior citizens.

Credit cards: If you have accumulated credit card

debts, pay them off, no matter how long it takes. Cut up the credit cards or stick them in a drawer to curtail spending when you don't have extra money, and live by this rule: If you can't pay for it with cash, you can't afford it!

If the current credit card you have a debt on has a high interest rate—of 18 percent or so—try to convert that debt to a credit card with a lower interest rate. To get customers, many card companies are offering low-teen or single-digit percentages and "no annual fee." For a list of these companies, check the financial magazines and the financial section of your newspaper.

Make sure the credit card you are using, or are about to secure, has at least a twenty-five-day grace period. This gives you twenty-five days from the time you make a purchase until interest begins to accumulate. If you pay your bills off monthly, you have free use of their money for twenty-five days.

And while you are at it, look for a card that will help you accumulate air mileage. It is a great way to earn a free trip while minimizing expenses.

EVERY PENNY COUNTS

If you have your "mad money" sitting in a checking account where it earns no interest, why not put that extra money in a credit union account or some other interest-bearing account until you need it?

INSURANCE POLICIES

Most individuals are paying for life insurance policies they don't really need. This can be an unnecessary expense as you get older, as well as draining on the retirement budget. Insurance wasn't meant to be a permanent need. For the most part, it is intended to protect younger families with fewer assets. As you grow older and accumulate assets, these assets replace the need for a life insurance policy.

Often, older people have paid into the policy far more than they will ever get from the policy. Also, this is giving away interest that could be earned. If you are in a retirement situation, ask yourself if you really need the insurance. If you do not, wouldn't it be better to take the money from the policy and invest it? You could conceivably accumulate more money with an investment of this money than what the death benefit will be.

Gerrard has a modest policy of $10,000, for which he pays $19 a month. He has been paying $19 a month for the past twenty years. At 35, he thought this was a great deal. Gerrard, now only fifty-five years old, is in excellent health. According to the life expectancy tables, he should be around for twenty-five more years. He has already paid $4560 into his policy. In the next 25 years, he will have paid another $5,700, for a grand total of $10,260 (this does not take into account any accumulated interest). He will have paid more than the policy will pay for him! He might as well have put that $19 a month under his mattress. If Gerrard had saved that $19 a month for the total forty-five years at an average interest rate of 5%, it would be worth $38,502.

It is with good reason that insurance companies are in the business of selling insurance: They make more money than they pay out.

A word of caution, though, for retired individuals: Before you ever cancel an insurance policy, make sure you are in *perfect health*. If you have any life-threatening illnesses, it is not advisable to cancel a policy that is in effect. *Consult with a professional advisor before you do anything.*

ADDITIONAL LIFE INSURANCE POLICIES

Do you have insurance policies on your children? What do you have them for? If there is not a good reason (and I would be hard-pressed to think of one), get rid of the policies and the additional payments. If you originally gave your child a policy as a gift, wouldn't it be better to give your child the cash or invest that money for growth?

REDUCE PREMIUMS ON CAR AND HOMEOWNERS INSURANCE

Take a good look at all your insurance policies. You may be able to save quite a bit of money by raising the deductible amount. Take the time to ask your insurance agent if there is anything you can safely do to lower your premium.

DON'T HAVE TAXES WITHHELD FROM YOUR PENSION PAYMENTS

Is anyone out there willing to loan the IRS money interest-free for the rest of their lives? If you are receiving a monthly pension and are having taxes withheld for you, then you are doing just that.

Morry has $300 a month withheld from his pension check for his taxes; $300 a month is $3,600 a year. Essentially Morry is giving the IRS an interest-free loan, and has been for the past twenty-nine years. Once you are no longer an employee, you are not required to have taxes withheld monthly from your pension check; you can pay your own taxes, or what is called estimated taxes.

Four times a year you are responsible for sending in a check to the IRS for the amount you owe in estimated taxes. Whoever does your taxes for you will figure out exactly how much you owe and prepare voucher slips with the correct amount indicated on them.

Rather than the IRS having access to this money interest-free, these funds could be sitting in your account earning interest for you. This may not seem like a lot of money to you, but over your life span it could add up to a considerable amount.

WHO SHOULD NOT PAY ESTIMATED TAXES?

If you are a spender rather than a saver, simply continue having taxes withheld.

SOCIAL SECURITY

The majority of you should plan to take Social Security when you are sixty-two instead of waiting until you reach sixty-five. Here's why:

If you are entitled to $1,000 a month at age sixty-five and only $800 a month at sixty-two, believe it or not, you could be losing money if you wait until sixty-five. For thirty-six months, from sixty-two to sixty-five, you will receive $28,800 ($800 × 36). If you wait until sixty-five to take the $1,000-a-month payment, that will be $200 more a month than if you had taken Social Security at age sixty-two. The question is: At sixty-five, how long would it take to save $28,800 if you put away $200 a month? The answer is twelve years (not including any interest that money could have earned). By taking Social Security at sixty-two, you have received this money in three years, not twelve.

Another way to look at it is to take the $800 a month and save it. In three years you will have saved about

$30,000, including interest. If you take this money and invest it at 6 percent, you will receive an income of $150 a month. This, added to your monthly Social Security payment of $800, is $950. That's only $50 less than the $1,000 you would receive from Social Security if you had waited until age sixty-five. The difference, of course, is that although you may be receiving $50 a month less, you have $30,000 in the bank. If interest rates climb to 10 percent, for instance, your income on the $30,000 will also increase. In this case it will be $250 a month. When added to your Social Security benefit of $800 a month, you will receive $1,050, or $50 more than if you had waited. So no matter how you look at it, by taking your Social Security at age sixty-two, you come out ahead.

WORKING AFTER SOCIAL SECURITY BEGINS

What if you decide to go back to work after you have begun to take your Social Security at age sixty-two? What you need to be careful about is that in 1998, for example, for any amount you make over $9,120* between ages sixty-two and sixty-five, Social Security will deduct $1 for every $2 you make. If you are between ages sixty-five and seventy, they will withhold $1 for every $3 you make over $14,500*. At age seventy or older, you can make any amount without any amount being withheld from your Social Security.

But here's what you can do about it. You are sixty-two and begin to collect Social Security benefits ($800 a month). A few months later, you decide to go back to work. You get a job that pays you $25,000 a year,

*Congress has the right to adjust this amount annually.

and you have totally disqualified yourself from receiving Social Security. You now have two options: One is that Social Security will place you on "work suspense," where you will not receive benefits but do receive work credits. These work credits are then recomputed to determine your new Social Security payment when you stop working. The second is that you can simply withdraw your social security application and repay everything they have paid you to date. *No interest will be owed on this money when you pay it back.* So you could have been collecting $800 a month, put it in the bank, and earned interest. If you had gotten a job at sixty-three that disqualifies you from receiving benefits, you can pay back the money and keep the interest. *Social Security gave you an interest-free loan.* By withdrawing your application, paying back the money, and reapplying at age sixty-five, you will receive your full benefit, or $1,000 a month, which is more than you would receive if you had gone on "work suspense."

SURVIVOR AND DIVORCE BENEFITS

Widowed:

Many widows and widowers receive their deceased spouse's Social Security benefits. But you must be sixty to apply (fifty if you are disabled), must have been married to the deceased for at least nine months at the time of his or her death, and *must be unmarried at the time you apply* or you will not be eligible for survivor benefits. If you remarry after you have applied you will not lose the benefits. If you had remarried prior to sixty, you must wait until you are sixty-one or older to apply for the deceased's benefits. If you are close to 60 and planning to remarry, wait until after you receive the benefits to get married.

Divorced/Widowed:

If you are divorced from your spouse and he or she dies, you will be entitled to survivor benefits if you had been married to him or her for at least ten years. The rules for applying for benefits are the same as above, except for the length of the marriage. You can remarry after receiving the benefits and retain them. When applying for Social Security benefits, however, compare to see which is the best deal: yours, your ex-spouse's, or your current spouse's.

Divorced:

If you are divorced from your spouse and he or she is still alive, to collect benefits you must be sixty-two years of age when you apply, have been married to him or her for at least ten years, and be unmarried at the time you apply. Should you remarry after receiving these benefits, you will not be entitled to further benefits from the first spouse. If you divorce again, you can return to receiving benefits from the first spouse if these benefits are higher or from the second spouse if you meet the application requirements above.

To call Social Security: 800-772-1213

PAYING OFF YOUR HOME BY SOCIAL SECURITY TIME

Your goal should ultimately be to pay off your home by the time you begin to receive Social Security. Your expenses will be reduced by the amount of the mortgage payment, and your income will be increased by your Social Security benefit. This could be a nice boost to your financial situation and help counter any effects on inflation. You can ask your mortgage company to provide you with a schedule of monthly payments based on how much you owe and the number of years until you reach sixty-two.

LONG-TERM CARE

If you want to safeguard your money, make sure to read Chapter Five, by far the most consequential chapter in this book.

ASSET RICH/CASH POOR: USING THE CHARITABLE REMAINDER TRUST

You may find yourself sitting on stock and/or real estate you cannot afford to sell because the taxes you would owe on their appreciated value are just too prohibitive.

You could set up a charitable remainder trust and gift this stock/real estate to a charity of your choice. Not only will you get a tax write-off for the next five years, but also you can receive a income from the donated gift. Upon the death of both partners, the charity receives the money. Basically, you have given away ownership of your funds, but not control of how they are invested or the income from those investments.

John and Darlene own a piece of land that they inherited years ago, when Johns father died. When they inherited the land it was worth $10,000. It has since appreciated in value to about $800,000. There is no income that is generated from this land. In fact, it costs John and Darlene $3,000 year in property taxes. If they were to sell the land now they would lose about 30 percent to the government in taxes, or about $240,000.

Even though John and Darlene really could use some extra income, they felt that that was too much to give up in taxes. Their option would be to gift the land to a charity *via* a trust. The charity could sell the land and not be obliged to pay the government any taxes because of their nonprofit status.

Now the charitable remainder trust can invest all

$800,000 to generate income for John and Darlene for the rest of their lives. Upon their deaths, the $800,000 becomes the sole property of the charity. The benefits to John and Darlene are twofold: One is a tax write-off, which will save them a considerable sum of money over the next few years; and they were able to move all of the $800,000 into an investment that will generate them a considerable sum of income. Remember, if they had sold the land on their own they would have to give up 30 percent in taxes, which would leave only $560,000 to generate income.

With the excess income, John and Darlene could purchase an insurance policy to replace the $800,000, so their children would not lose out. In fact, if it is set up correctly, the children will also benefit by not having to pay estate tax on the life insurance proceeds; they will get to keep all $800,000. If they were to inherit the land, chances are they would have a nice estate tax bill to pay (see Chapter Two).

A good estate planning lawyer should be able to answer all the questions you have concerning a charitable remainder trust.

The sooner you take action on the above suggestions that are appropriate for you, the better off you will be financially. The better off you are financially, the less stress you will have in your life, and you will be able to enjoy your retirement. Then the title to your own real-life chapter will be "Minimize Worry and Maximize Enjoyment."

chapter 9

A Successful Retirement

Your Story

This is where we leave off and the plans for your successful retirement begin. Through Anita, Marcia, Barbara, Anna, Shirley, Doug, and the others, it is our hope that we have communicated the importance of taking the necessary steps to protect your assets, your family and your retirement.

Have a great retirement!

GLOSSARY

actuaries   Professionals who work for insurance companies and evaluate your application and medical records to project how long you will live.

advance directive   A document that expresses your general wishes about critical care but does not authorize anyone to act on your behalf or make decisions the way a durable power of attorney for health care does.

annuity   A series of fixed-amount payments paid at regular intervals over the specified period of the annuity.

arbitration   An informal hearing held regarding a dispute. The dispute is judged by a group of people (generally three) who have been selected by an impartial panel. Once a decision has been reached, there is no appeal process with arbitration. The process is faster and less costly than going to court.

asset   A resoursce that has economic value to its owner. Examples are cash, accounts receivable, inventory, real estate, securities.

asset allocation   Dividing your investment portfolio among the major asset categories.

blue chip stock   A term used for the stock of a large, well-known company.

bonds   Investments that are considered debt investments—for example, you are loaning money to an entity that needs funds for a defined period of time at a specified interest rate. In exchange for your money, the entity will issue you a certificate, or bond, that states the interest rate you are to be paid and when your funds are to be returned to you, or the maturity date of the bond. Interest on bonds is paid every six months.

corporate bond   A bond issued by a corporation (see bonds)

municipal bond   A bond issued by a municipality and that generally is tax-free—you pay no taxes on the interest you earn. Because it is tax-free, the interest rate is usually lower than for a taxable bond.

Treasury bond   A bond issued by the U.S. government. These are considered safe investments because they are backed by the taxing authority of the U.S. government. The interest on Treasury bonds is not subject to state income tax. Such a bond is usually held for seven or more years.

Treasury note   The only difference is that a Treasury note is issued for a shorter time (e.g., two to five years) than a Treasury bond (q.v.).

Treasury bill   This is held for a shorter time (e.g., three, six, or nine months to two years) than either a Treasury bond (q.v.) or a Treasury note (q.v.). Interest on T-bills are paid at the time the bill matures, and the bills are priced accordingly.

zero coupon bonds   A bond that generates no periodic interest payments and is issued at a discount from face value. The Return is realized at maturity.

cash investment   Short-term obligation, usually ninety days or less, that provides a return in the form of interest payments. Examples are money-market funds and short-term CD's.

certificate of deposit (CD)   A savings certificate entitling the bearer to receive interest. CDs are generally issued by commercial banks and savings and loans.

certified financial planner   A person who is certified to give financial advice. One must study and take extensive exams in the following areas to become certified: financial planning, taxes, insurance, estate planning, and retirement. Continuing education credits are required each year to maintain the certification status.

COBRA   Consolidated Omnibus Budget Reconciliation Act of 1985. If your company is covered by a COBRA plan and you leave your job for whatever reason and were an active participant in the company's health plan prior to your departure date, you have the right, if you wish, to continue the health insurance coverage you and your family received, for at least eighteen months. You will have to pay for this coverage out of your own pocket, but it cannot be more than 102 percent of the normal cost of coverage. COBRA is meant to protect you while you look for another policy.

commission   Broker's fee for buying or selling securities.

conservatorship   A circumstance in which the court declares an individual unable to take care of legal matters and appoints another individual, known as a conservator, to do so.

custodial care   Refers to a particular level of care an individual may need. Help in eating, toileting, bathing, dressing, etc.—any activities that usually do not require a professional such as a nurse or a therapist.

defined benefit pension plan   A retirement plan based on a formula that indicates the exact benefit that one can expect upon retiring. There are restrictions as to when and how you can withdraw these funds without penalties.

defined contribution plan   A retirement plan wherein a certain amount or percentage of money is set aside each year for the benefit of the employee. There is no way to know how much that will ultimately give the employee upon retiring. There are restrictions as to when and how you can withdraw these funds without penalties.

discount broker   A stockbroker who charges a reduced commission and provides no investment advice.

dividend   A cash payment, financed by profits, that is designated by the company's board of directors to distribute among stockholders.

Dow Jones industrial average (DJIA)   The price average of thirty actively traded blue chip stocks.

equity   Another word for stock or similar ownership securities.

estate   An estate consists of those things you own of value, such as real estate, art collections, collectibles, antiques, jewelry, investments, and life insurance.

estate tax   A tax levied on your estate or valuables on any amount currently over $600,000. This tax does not apply between spouses, who can leave any amount to one another upon death—known as the unlimited marital deduction. It is upon the death of the surviving spouse that estate taxes may be owed.

financial planner   An investment professional who helps individuals delineate financial plans with specific objectives and helps coordinate various financial activities.

fixed-income security An investment that provides a return in the form of fixed periodic payments and return of principle. Examples are bonds and CDs.

401K A voluntary retirement plan offered to employees of a company that allows up to a certain percentage of their pretax pay to be set aside and invested within the retirement plan. The percentage varies from company to company and can increase each year. The employer can also contribute to the employees' plan if they wish. The funds and the growth are not taxed until the funds are withdrawn. There are restrictions as to when and how you can withdraw these funds without penalties.

gatekeeper This term can be alternately used with *qualifiers*. For a long-term-care policy to begin paying benefits, you must qualify for these benefits. To qualify, you must meet certain standards, gatekeepers.

growth stock Shares of a company whose total earnings are expected to grow at an above average rate.

income stock Stocks having a history of regular dividend payments that contribute to the largest portion of the stock's overall return.

investment advisor A person who manages assets, making portfolio composition and individual security selection decisions for a fee, usually a percentage of assets invested.

IRA (individual retirement account) A retirement account set up at a bank, credit union, brokerage firm, insurance company, or mutual fund company that allows a yearly contribution, not to exceed $2,000, for the individual working person. Married couples, where one spouse works and the other does not, may contribute a maximum, combined contribution of $4,000.

The contributions are tax-deductible if you are not currently covered by a 401K or pension plan at your place of employment. If you are covered by a pension plan, how much income you earn will determine the tax-deductibility of the IRA. Check with a tax advisor. There are restrictions as to when and how you can withdraw these funds without penalties.

IRA rollover   An account used to transfer retirement funds currently being held in a company retirement plan where taxes continue to be deferred. Simply stated, the funds are "rolled" from their current plan into an IRA rollover account. There are restrictions as to when and how you can withdraw or transfer these funds without penalties or taxes.

Keogh/HR10   A retirement plan set up by self-employed individuals who are not incorporated. The self-employed individual is allowed to make a tax-deductible contribution up to a certain percentage of his or her income. The funds grow without taxation until they are withdrawn. This type of retirement plan is eligible for forward-averaging taxation. There are restrictions as to when and how you can withdraw these funds without penalties.

liquidity   The degree of ease and certainty of value with which a security can be converted to cash.

living will   See advance directive.

long-term care   Any type of health or medical support or care needed over an extended period.

Medicaid   A federal- and state-government-funded program that pays for long-term care, medical bills, and some health care services for extremely-low-income individuals. Considered a form of welfare.

MediCal The name for Medicaid in the state of California.

Medicare A federally instituted medical care program that provides medical and hospital insurance for those who are sixty-five or older or for those who are disabled.

Medigap insurance An insurance policy individually purchased to cover gaps in Medicare, such as copayments and deductibles.

mutual fund A professionally managed pool of monies to buy stocks, bonds, etc. Each mutual fund is sold under a legal document called a prospectus, which explains the objective of the fund, all fees and expenses involved, and guidelines the fund must abide by when investing your money. Always read the prospectus before investing.

  class A shares of a mutual fund See loaded mutual fund.
  class B shares of a mutual fund A mutual fund that does not charge an up-front purchase fee, but does have a redemption fee upon leaving the fund or family of funds before a certain length of time. The fee amount generally starts at 5 percent and declines to 1 percent as time goes on. This is not to be confused with a no-load fund.
  loaded mutual fund A mutual fund that has a fee to purchase it. The fee could be 4½ percent or more.
  no-load mutual fund A mutual fund that has no fee to buy or sell it.

National Association of Securities Dealers Automated Quotations system (NASDAQ) Computerized system that provides up-to-the-minute price quotations on some 5,000 of the more actively traded over-the-counter stocks.

New York Stock Exchange index   A market value–weighted measure of stock market changes for all stocks listed on the NYSE.

open-end fund   A mutual fund that continues to sell shares to investors and will buy back shares when investors wish to sell. Open-end funds have no limit to the number of shares they can issue.

option   A privilege sold by one party to another that offers the buyer the right to buy (call) or sell (put) a security at an agreed-upon price during a certain period of time or on a specific date. Buying options are speculative and risky.

over-the-counter market   A communications network through which trades of bonds, non-listed stocks, and other securities take place. The trading is overseen by the National Association of Securities Dealers (NASD).

pension plan   A retirement plan wherein the employer makes contributions for the employee. Many are being replaced by the 401K. There are restrictions as to when and how you can withdraw these funds without penalties.

points   When refinancing, the amount you pay the lender at the closing of the loan. Each point is equal to 1 percent of the mortgage loan.

pop-up option   A joint and survivor option that allows you to be reinstated to the basic pension amount if the spouse predeceases the retiree. More and more companies are utilizing this option for an additional charge. Generally, this pop-up option is limited to married couples.

profit-sharing plan   A plan wherein the employees

get a share in the profits of the company. The company decides what portion of the profit will be shared. Each employee then receives, into an account, a percentage of those profits based on their earnings. There are restrictions as to when and how you can withdraw these funds without penalties.

prospectus   See mutual fund.

registered investment advisor (RIA)   An advisor who usually manages money for a fee or commissions. This individual is registered with the Department of Corporations in the state in which he or she practices as well as with the Securities and Exchange Commission for a federal registration.

SEP/IRA (simplified employee plan/individual retirement account)   A retirement plan for employers with few or no employees. It works like an IRA in that the employee will have ownership to this account but the employer funds it. There are restrictions as to when and how you can withdraw these funds without penalties.

severance   When a company lets an employee go, it may offer compensation for being severed. Severance usually is handled as a normal paycheck with all the standard taxes withheld.

skilled care   Skilled care is medical care that can be performed only by or under the supervision of licensed nursing personnel under instructions of a physician.

Standard & Poor's 500 index   A market value–weighted index of 500 major U.S. corporations that includes 400 industrial firms, 20 transportation firms, 40 utilities, and 40 financial firms.

stockbroker   A person who buys or sells stocks, bonds,

or other investments for another individual. Most stockbrokers work on a commission or fee basis. They are licensed by one or more government agencies, which monitor and regulate their activities.

stocks   Stocks are considered an equity investment; in other words, you own shares, or stock, in a company. The value of these shares can go up or down.

> **common stock**   A security representing ownership issued by a corporation.
>
> **preferred stock**   A security which represents a claim prior to common stock on the firm's earnings and assets. Preferred stockholders generally forgo voting rights and receive a fixed dividend that takes precedence over payment of dividends to common stockholders.

stock dividend   A dividend paid in additional shares of stock rather than in cash.

stock split   The division of a company's existing stock into more shares. In a two-for-one split, each stockholder would receive an additional share for each share already held.

suitability   A determination of whether a trading strategy is in line with an investor's financial means and investment objectives.

tax-sheltered annuity (TSA)   A retirement account for certain workers such as teachers and hospital employees. A voluntary percentage, up to a maximum amount, is taken from pretax dollars and set aside for the employee. TSAs usually are held with insurance companies, where the money is placed in fixed accounts to earn interest. There are restrictions as to when and how you can withdraw these funds without penalties.

term life insurance   Insurance that is good for a specific amount of time is referred to as term insurance. It may be good for a year, five years, ten years, or whatever, and is considerably less expensive when purchased during those years when insurance companies statistically don't expect you to die. When the term on the insurance runs out, the policy is repriced according to your age. The older you are, the greater the cost becomes.

unlimited marital deduction   A deceased husband or wife can pass assets to the other without any estate tax owed.

Value Line index   An index of 1,700 companies from the New York and American Stock Exchanges and the over-the-counter-market. As an equal-weighted index, each of the 1,700 stocks has equal effect, regardless of price or total market value.

whole life insurance   An insurance policy that will cover you for your whole life, no matter how long that happens to be. Because this is maximum coverage, it is also more expensive than term life insurance.

Wilshire 5000 equity index   A stock market measure of some 5,000 equity securities, including all New York Stock Exchange and American Stock Exchange issues and the most active over-the-counter issues. The index represents the total dollar value of all 5,000 stocks.

RESOURCES

All books listed can be purchased or ordered through your local bookstore, even though we have listed publishers' addresses and phone numbers.

AARP publications may be obtained by contacting:

AARP Fulfillment
601 E Street, NW
Washington, D.C. 20049
Tel.: 800-424-3410

Be sure to place the publication code on the outside envelope and on your request.

The following brochures are free, except where noted. Book prices are listed but may change. Check with your bookseller or the publisher.

CHAPTER ONE

Associations and brochures:

NASD (National Association of Securities Dealers)
1390 Piccard Drive
Rockville, MD 20850
Tel.: 301-590-6500
Ask for a catalog of publications

SEC (Securities and Exchange Commission)
Office of Consumer Affairs
450 Fifth Street, NW, Room 2111

Mail Stop 2-6
Washington, DC 20549
Tel.: 202-272-7440; 202-272-7065 (telecommuni-
cations for the deaf)
Free brochures:

- *How to Proceed with Arbitration of a Small Claim*
- *Arbitration Procedures*
- *Code of Arbitration Procedures*

Commodity Futures Trading Commission
Division of Enforcement
2033 K Street, NW, Suite 600
Washington, DC 20581
Tel.: 202-254-7424

To obtain lists of investment managers and advisors:

Investment Counsel Association of America
20 Exchange Place
New York, NY 10005
Tel.: 212-344-0999

To obtain lists of Certified Financial Planners:

Institute of Certified Financial Planners
7600 East Eastman Avenue, Suite 301
Denver, CO 80231-4397
Tel.: 800-282-7526 or 303-751-7600

For a list of chartered financial consultants (CFC):

American College
270 Bryn Mawr Avenue
Bryn Mawr, PA 19010
Tel.: 215-526-1000

For a free referral to Registered Financial Planning practitioners in your area or for a copy of *The Registry of Financial Planning Directory* ($2.50).*

> International Association for Financial Planning
> 5775 Glenridge Drive, N.E., Suite B, #300
> Atlanta, GA 30328-5364
> Tel.: 404-845-0011

For CPA/Personal Financial Planners:

> American Institute of Certified Public Accountants
> Personal Financial Planning Division
> Harborside Financial Center
> 201 Plaza 3
> Jersey City, NJ 07311
> Tel.: 800-862-4272

> LINC, Inc. (Licensed Independent Network of CPA Financial Planners)
> 404 James Robertson Pkwy, Suite 1200
> Nashville, TN 37219
> Tel.: 615-242-7351

Free brochures and referrals in your area:

> National Association of Personal Financial Advisors
> 355 West Dundee Road, Suite 200
> Buffalo Grove, IL 60089
> Tel: 888-FEE-ONLY   (888-333-6659)

---

*Registered financial planning practitioners must have three years' experience, pass extensive written exams, have a related degree, and have references from at least five clients. Currently only 5 percent of members of this organization have earned this designation.

Money Matters: How to Talk to and Select Financial Planners (Publication D12380)

> AARP Fulfillment
> 601 E Street, NW
> Washington, DC 20049
> Tel.: 800-424-3410

For a brochure on tips on selecting a stockbroker, send a self-addressed, stamped envelope to:

> Council of Better Business Bureaus
> 4200 Wilson Boulevard
> Arlington, VA 22203
> Tel.: 703-276-0100

For a list of discount brokers:

> *An Individual Investor's Guide to Discount Brokers:*
> American Association of Individual Investors
> 625 N. Michigan Ave., Suite 1900
> Chicago, IL 60611
> Tel.: 312-280-0170

Information on the Internet:

> Investment Brokerages Guide
> http://www.cs.cmu.edu/~jdg/invest_brokers/index.html

Book:
Allen, John Lawrence. *Investor Beware: How to Protect Your Money from Wall Street's Dirty Tricks.* New York: John Wiley & Sons, 1993.

For complaints:

- Call your state's Department of Consumer Protection Agencies, listed in your telephone book under "Government." Call these agencies for additional help and information.
- Call your local Better Business Bureau.

To learn more about investing on your own:

Join an investment club. At the forefront of the movement since 1951, the NAIC (National Association of Investors Corporation) philosophy is empowerment through education. They offer tools for clubs and individuals by providing materials, publications, software, a low cost investment plan for DRPs, a mutual fund, investment seminars and fairs, an Investor Advisory Service, and their own magazine *Better Investing*.

NAIC (National Association of Investors
Corporation)
P.O. Box 220
Royal Oak, MI 48068
Tel.: 810-583-6242
Fax: 810-583-4880

American Association of Individual Investors
625 N. Michigan Avenue
Chicago, IL 60611-3110
Tel.: 312-280-0170

website address: http://www.aaii.org/

This is an information-only organization. They provide no services. *AAII Journal* comes out ten times a year.

To invest directly with dividend reinvestment programs (DRPs):

NAIC (see previous)

First Share
P.O.Box 222
Westcliffe, CO 81252
Tel.: 719-783-2929

First Share offers DRP opportunities with 850 companies. Through them you can buy one share of a stock for a nominal fee and be set up to invest directly with the company afterward.

General publications to learn more about investing:

These publications may be ordered directly, purchased from newsstands, or obtained from your local library.

AAII Journal: American Association of Individual Investors, 625 N. Michigan Avenue, Chicago, IL 60611. Tel.: 312-280 0170. $49 /year for ten issues. Among the articles are: "Low Load Guide to Mutual Funds" (March); "Guide to Dividend Reinvestment Plans" (June); "Personal Tax and Financial Planner Guide" (Dec).

Better Investing: NAIC, P.O. Box 220, Royal Oak, MI 48068, Tel.: 810-583-6242; Fax: 810-583-4880. (monthly) $24 /year

Barron's: Dow Jones & Co., 200 Burnett Road, Chicopee MA 01020. Tel.: 800-568-7625 (weekly). Thirteen weeks/$37; twenty-six weeks/$71; fifty-two weeks/$140.

Investor's Business Daily: Investor's Business Daily, Inc., P.O. Box 661750, Los Angeles, CA 90066. Tel.: 800-831-2525 (five days a week). Six months/ $103; one year/$189.

*Kiplinger's Personal Finance Magazine:*1729 H Street, NW, Washington, DC 20006. Tel.: 800-544-0155 (monthly). $19.95 per year.

Forbes: Forbes Inc., 60 Fifth Avenue, New York, NY 10011. Tel.: 800-888-9896. (biweekly) $57 per year.

Money Magazine: P. O. Box 60001, Tampa, FL 33660. Tel.: 800-541-1000. (monthly). 13 issues/$39.95. Special issues include mutual funds ranking guide.

Standard & Poor's Guides: Standard & Poor's Corporation, 25 Broadway, New York, NY 10004. Tel.: 800-221-7940. Among the most useful journals are :

> *S&P Bond Guide* (monthly)
> *S&P Directory of Dividend Reinvestment Plans* (annual)
> *S&P Stock Guide* (monthly)
> *S&P Stock Report* (quarterly)

Value Line Investment Survey: Rating and Reports and *Selection and Opinions*; (two vols.): Value Line Publishing, 220 East 42nd Street, New York, NY 10017. Tel.: 800-634-3583. (weekly updates) $570 per year.

Wall Street Journal: Dow Jones & Company, Inc., 200 Burnett Road, Chicopee, MA 01020. Tel.: 800-568-7625. (five times a week) thirteen weeks/$49; twenty-six weeks/$89; one year/$175.

Investment and Financial Information on the Internet:

CNNfn	http://cnnfn.com
EDGAR	http://www.sec.gov/edgarhp.htm
INVESTools	http://www.investools.com
American Stock Exchange	http://www.amex.com/
The Silicon Investor	http://www.techstocks.com/

Wall Street Journal   http://update.wsj.com/
Interactive   welcome.html
AAII Web Site   http://www.aaii.org/

Mutual Fund Information on the Internet:

NETworth   http://networth.galt.com/
Mutual Funds Magazine   http://www.mfmag.com/
Mutual Funds Interactive   http://www.brill.com

For Tax Information:

Internal Revenue Service
    http://www.irs.ustreas.gov/prod/cover.html
IRS Forms and Publications:
    http://www.irs.ustreas.gov/prodformd__pubs/
index.html

Essential Links to Taxes
    http://www.el.com/ToTheWeb/Taxes/

CHAPTERS TWO AND THREE

Associations:

Send letter requesting referrals for your area:

American College of Trust and Estate Counsel
3415 South Sepulveda Boulevard, Suite 60
Los Angeles, CA 90034
Tel.: 310-398-1888

Books:

Berg, Adriane G. *Gifting to People You Love: The Complete Guide to Making Gifts, Bequests, and Investments for Children*. New York: Newmarket Press, 1996.

Clifford, Denis. *Make Your Own Living Trust*. Berkeley, CA: Nolo Press, 1993. (950 Parker Street, Berkeley, CA 94710. Tel.: 800-992-6656*)

A resource for understanding trusts and back-up wills. But we still recommend seeking counsel from a reputable trust lawyer.

Clifford, Denis. *Plan Your Estate*. Berkeley, CA: Nolo Press, 1992.

Clifford, Denis. *Simple Will Book: How To Prepare a Legally Valid Will*, 2nd Ed. Berkeley, CA: Nolo Press, 1995.

Write or call Nolo Press for an order form and list of available books and software. See bottom of page 213.

Schumacher, Vickie and Jim. *Understanding Living Trusts*. Los Angeles: Schumacher & Company, 1990. (1800 Century Park East, Suite 1250, Los Angeles, CA 90067. Tel.: 310-859-0800)

CHAPTER FOUR

Brochures:

For *Tomorrow's Choices: Preparing Now for Future Legal, Financial, and Health Care Decisions* (D13479) and *Health Care Powers of Attorney* (D13895):

> AARP Fulfillment
> 601 E Street, NW
> Washington, DC 20049
> Tel.: 800-424-3410

Books:

Clifford, Denis. *The Power of Attorney Book*. Berkeley, CA: Nolo Press, 1991.

Older Women's League. *Taking Charge of the End of Your Life*. 730 Eleventh Street, NW, Suite 300 Washington, DC 20001
Tel.: 202-783-6686

CHAPTER FIVE

The insurance rating services and their telephone numbers:

A. M. Best	908-439-2200
Standard & Poor's	212-208-8000
Moody's	212-553-0377
Duff & Phelps	312-263-2610
Weiss	800-289-8100 (except Florida); 407-627-3300 (there is a $15 telephone or $45 written evaluation-charge for ratings from this service)

Information on the Internet:

Insurance News Network:	http://www.insure.com
Independent Insurance Network	http:// www.iiaa.iix.com/ default.htm

Associations:

National Council on Aging
409 3rd Street, SW
Suite 200
Washington, DC 20024
Tel.: 202-479-1200

Health Insurance Association of America
1001 Pennsylvania Avenue, NW
Washington, DC 20004-2599
Tel.: 800-942-4242

Brochures:

Before You Buy: A Guide to LTC Insurance (D12893)

AARP Fulfillment
601 E Street, NW
Washington, DC 20049
Tel.: 800-424-3410

For a copy of *Consumer's Guide to LTC Insurance:*

Health Insurance Association of America
1001 Pennsylvania Avenue, NW
Washington, DC 20004
Tel.: 800-432-8000

For a list of available brochures for California residents:

California Advocates for Nursing Home Reform
1610 Bush Street
San Francisco, CA 94109
Tel.: 415-474-5171

For a copy of *Shopper's Guide to Long-Term-Care Insurance:*

National Association of Insurance Commissioners
120 West 12th Street
Kansas City, MO 64105
Tel.: 816-842-3600

Books:

Gordon, Harley. *How To Protect Your Life Savings from Catastrophic Illness and Nursing Homes.* Boston: FSP (Financial Strategies Press), 1994.

Matthews, Joseph. *Elder Care.* Emeryville, CA: Nolo Press, 1990.

Palla, Susan E., and Barry G. Eldridge. *Insider's Guide to Long-Term Care.* Parsippany, NJ: Individual and Commercial Administrators, 1992. (9 Sylvan Way, Suite 170, Parsippany, NJ 07054. Tel.: 800-422-0696).

United Seniors Health Cooperative. *Long Term Care: A Dollar and Sense Guide.* Washington, DC, 1994. (1331 H Street, NW, Washington, DC 20005. Tel.: 202-393-6222).

CHAPTERS SIX AND SEVEN

Associations and brochures:

> *Your Pension: Things You Should Know About Your Pension Plan*
> Pension Benefit Guarantee Corp.
> 2020 K Street, NW
> Washington, DC 20006

> *Protect Yourself: A Woman's Guide to Pension Rights* (D12258); *Guide to Understanding Your Pension Plan* (D13533)
> AARP Fulfillment
> 601 E Street, NW
> Washington, DC 20049
> Tel.: 800-424-3410

Free IRS publications can be obtained from any IRS office, on line, or by calling 800-424-3676. *Individual Retirement Arrangements* (Publication 590) can be obtained from the IRS.

Free government brochures can be obtained from any local Social Security office, or by calling 800-772-1213 for the following:

- *How Your Retirement Benefit Is Figured* (Publication 05–10070)
- *Understanding Social Security* (Publication 05–10024)
- *The Appeals Process* (Publication 05–10035)

- *Retirement* (Publication 05–10035)
- *When You Get Social Security Retirement or Survivor Benefits: What You Need to Know* (Publication 05–10077)

Social Security On Line: http://www.ssa.gov

To get insurance rate quotes:

For rates on term life insurance from different companies:

Select Quote Insurance Services
140 Second Street
San Francisco, CA 94105
Tel.: 800-343-1985

To obtain a quote for a competitively priced whole-life insurance policy:

USAA Life
Tel.: 800-531-8000

Quote Services on Line:

InsuranceQuote Services (800-972-1104)	http://www.iquote.com
MasterQuote (800-337-5433)	http:// www.masterquote.com
QuickQuote (800-867-2404)	http:// www.quickquote.com
Quotesmith (800-431-1147)	http:// www.quotesmith.com
TermQuote (800-444-8376)	http://http:// www.reinet.com/ termquote

Article:

Topolnicki, Denise. "Go from Pink Slip to Paycheck," *Money*, March 1994.

Books:

Korn, Donald J. *Your Money or Your Life.* New York: Macmillan, 1992.

Matthews, Joseph L. *Social Security, Medicare and Pensions,* 6th Ed. Berkeley, CA: Nolo Press, 1996.

CHAPTER EIGHT

For information on reverse mortgages:

> National Center for Home Equity Conversion
> 1210 E. College, Suite 200
> Marshall, MN 56258

For the publication *Home Made Money:*

> AARP/Home Equity Conversion Service
> 601 E Street, NW
> Washington, DC 20049
> Tel.: 800-424-3410

GENERAL RESOURCE BOOKS

Biracree, Tom and Nancy. *Over Fifty: The Resource Book for the Better Half of Your Life.* New York: HarperCollins, 1991.

Dychtwald, Ken, and Joe Flower. *Age Wave: The Challenges and Opportunities of an Aging America.* New York: Bantam Books, 1990.

Ottenbourg, Robert K. *Kiplinger's Retire and Thrive: Remarkable People Share Their Creative, Productive and Profitable Retirement Strategies.* Washington, DC: Kiplinger Press, 1995.

Quinn, Jane Bryant. *Making The Most of Your Money.* New York: Simon & Schuster, 1991.

INDEX

A

American College of Trust and Estate
    Counsel, The, 47–48
annuities, 152
    annuitization advice, 112
    life insurance with annuity, 151–53
asset calculations, 165–67
attorneys
    community service by, 44
    estate planning advice, 45–48, 193
    fees, 44–45, 46–47
    finding, 43–48
    gifting, advice in, 65, 66
    and Medicaid eligibility, 65
    services expected, 45–47
    for trust preparation, 34–36, 43–48, 193

B

banking rates, 184–85

C

charitable remainder trust, 192–93
checking accounts
    in trust, 37
children
    education of, 115
    gifting to. *See* gifting
    inheritance considerations. *See* trusts and
        wills
    life insurance on, 187
community property
    joint tenancy compared to, 60–61
conservatorships, 29, 53–54
Consolidated Omnibus Budget Reconcilia-
    tion Act of 1985 (COBRA), 117
credit cards, 163–64, 169, 171, 176–77,
    184–85

D

debt reorganization, 163–64
    asset calculations, 165–67
    bank rates, 184–85
    charitable remainder trust, use of, 192–93
    credit cards, 163–64, 169, 171, 176–77,
        184–85
    estimated taxes, payment of, 188
    insurance premium reductions, 187
    life insurance expenses, 185–87
    listing of debts, 164
    paying down debts
      with cash, 168
      friend or relative, loan from, 179–80
      "hardship case" reduction in mortgage
        interest, 180
      home equity loans, 175–78
      with investments, 168–69
      mortgage payoff, 179, 191
      refinancing home, 169–74, 178, 181,
        184
      rental property debt, 184
      replacement of assets, 169, 177
    pension payment withholding, 187–88
    rental property debt, 184
    reverse mortgages. *See* reverse mortgages
    spare cash, 185
dental insurance, 116–17
divorce
    joint tenancy and, 59–60
    Social Security for divorced surviving
      spouse, 191
durable power of attorney for
    health care (DPAHC), 47, 68–71
    backup agents, 74
    choosing your agent, 72–74
    clarity of intentions, 74–75

coagents, use of, 73–74
cost of, 77
defined, 70, 77
doctor and hospital agreement, 75
documentation, 75–77
importance of, 78
life support guidelines, 71–72
living will, compared to, 78
problems, anticipation of, 74
updating of, 77

E
early retirement, 2, 133–34
    education of children, 115
    emotional readiness for, 114–15, 133–34
    financial advisors regarding, 109, 110, 112, 113–14
    financial readiness for, 115–22
    health care considerations, 116–17
    home considerations, 116
    income calculations, 120–21
    monthly expenses calculation, 118–20
    retirement accounts
        access to, 106, 107–13
        calculations, 121–23
        IRA rollovers, 125–26, 129–30, 132–33
        leaving money in company plan, 125–26, 130–33
        options for funds, 125–33
        protection of funds, 123–24
        SEPP payments from, 108–13
        table of advantages and disadvantages, 132–33
        ten- or five-year averaging for taxes, 125, 127–29, 130, 131, 132, 133
        time pressures, 133
    spousal income, 114, 115, 120–21
    substantially equal periodic payments (SEPP) from retirement accounts, 108–9
        amount of, 109
        distribution method, 109–11
        "fifty-five or over" rule, 112–13
        investment for SEPP, 111–12
        length of time, 108

unemployment benefits, availability of, 120
    "voluntary" offers of, 104–7
emotions
    attitude toward money, 10, 14, 17
    early retirement, readiness for, 114–15, 133–34
    loneliness of surviving spouse, 139
estate planning. *See* specific subject headings
estate taxes, 22–25, 30, 39–43
    A-B or marital trusts to avoid, 25, 40–43
    gifting, problems of, 63–64
    and gift taxes, 52–53
    threshold for, 39–40, 41–42, 52–53
expenses. *See* monthly expenses

F
FDIC protection, 37
financial advisors, 2, 5–9. *See also* attorneys
    arbitration of losses, 8
    contracts, 16
    discretionary accounts, 19
    early retirement considerations, 109, 110, 112, 113–14
    emotional attitude toward money, 10, 14, 17
    evaluation of, 12–14
    fees and commissions, 14–16
    finding, 11–18
    gifting, advice on, 65, 66
    interview preparation and process, 10–18
    on life insurance alternatives, 153, 155, 156, 157
    monitoring account, 19–21
    National Association of Securities Dealers (NASD), 11, 18, 21
    opening account, 18–19
    registered investment advisors (RIAs), 14–17
    return and safety of investment, information on, 17, 20–21
    signing documents, 8, 16, 18–19

financial advisors (*cont.*)
  statements from, 16–17, 19
  trades, approval for, 20
  trusts vs. wills, on, 34–37
  verification of information from, 17–18
  wrap accounts, 16
401K plans, 106, 112
  substantially equal periodic payments
    (SEPP) from, 108–13

G
gifting
  children predeceasing parents, 62–63
  Medicaid, to qualify for, 62, 65–66
  probate, to avoid, 62, 64
  reasons for, 62, 66
  reverse mortgages, effect on, 66
  sale of gifted home, 64
  tax disadvantages of, 64, 65, 66
  trust advantages over, 63–67
gift taxes
  and gifting, 66–67
  and joint tenancy, 52–53
guardianship, 29–30

H
health insurance, 81
  COBRA program, 117
  dental and optical care insurance, 116–17
  durable power of attorney for health care
    (DPAHC), notification of, 77
  early retirement considerations, 116–17
  long-term-care (LTC) insurance. *See*
    long-term care
  maximum lifetime coverage, 70
  Medicaid. *See* Medicaid
  Medicare, 81, 83, 84–85
  Medigap policies, 83
  for surviving spouse, 140
home
  community property vs. joint tenancy,
    60–61
  cost-basis for tax purposes, 60–61, 64
  early retirement considerations, 116
  equity loans, 175–78

gifted home, sale of, 64
"hardship case" reduction in mortgage
  interest, 180
income taxes on sale of, 60–61, 64
joint tenancy, problems of, 54–56, 60–61
in Medicaid qualification, 65
paying off mortgage, 179, 191
refinancing, 169–74, 178, 181, 184
  costs of refinancing, 171–73
  home equity loans compared, 175–78
  reasons to refinance, 170–71
  rental property debt payment, 184
  tax deductions, 173
  trust, home in, 37
  years added to loan, 173–74
reverse mortgages, 54, 66, 181–84
selling home, 55, 60–61, 64, 178
Social Security time, paying off prior to,
  191
surviving spouse, as asset for, 135, 139,
  140
value of estate, 23–24, 41–42

I
income taxes
  for probate estate, 30
  on sale of home, 60–61, 64
  for trust, 39
incompetence
  joint tenancy, problems of, 53–54
  trust provision for, 47
insurance
  dental and optical care insurance, 116–17
  health insurance. *See* health insurance
  life insurance. *See* life insurance
  long-term-care (LTC) insurance. *See*
    long-term care
  premium reductions, 187
intestacy, 58
investments. *See also* financial
  advisors
  CDs, 11, 17
  and debt reorganization, 166, 168–69
  emotional attitude toward money, 10, 14,
    17

goals of, 10, 13–14, 17
joint and survivor benefit calculations,
    159–62
life insurance alternatives, 145–55
recordkeeping, 17–18, 19–21
returns, expected, 17, 20–21
risk, 10, 17
SEPP investments, 108–12. *See also* early
    retirement
IRAs, 113
    rollovers from company plans, 125–26,
        129–30, 132–33

J
joint and survivor benefits, 135–38
    advantages of, 145, 156–57
    disadvantages of, 144–45, 148–50
    increase in expenses for surviving spouse,
        138–40
    investment return calculations,
        159–62
    life insurance alternatives
        amount to purchase, 149–50, 152–53,
            155
        cost of policies, 151, 153, 155
        finding insurance company, 150–51
        term insurance coupled with invest-
            ment program, 146, 153–56
        when to purchase insurance, 156–58
        whole-life with investment of death
            proceeds, 145, 147–51
    options offered by companies, 135,
        137–38, 140–45, 158–62
    pop-up option, 144–45, 158
    women, involvement of, 140–41
joint tenancy WROS, 2, 25
    community property compared to, 60–61
    conservatorship, avoidance of, 53–54
    divorce and, 59–60
    and gift taxes, 52–53
    incompetence of joint tenant, 53–54
    lawsuits, effect of, 54
    parent/child joint tenancy, problems of,
        52–56
    reverse mortgages, effect on, 54

selling home, effect on, 55
tax consequences, 52–53
wills, overriding of, 49–51, 56–58

L
lawsuits, 54, 66, 76, 78
life insurance, 144–47
    alternatives to joint and survivor benefits
        amount of insurance, 149–50, 152–53,
            155
        cost of policies, 151, 153, 155
        finding insurance company, 150–51
        insurance and annuity, 146, 151–53
        term insurance coupled with invest-
            ment program, 146, 153–56
        when to purchase insurance, 156–58
        whole-life with investment of death
            proceeds, 145, 147–51
    cancellation of, 186
    on children, 187
    medical examination, 156, 186
    as unnecessary expense, 185–87
    when to purchase, 156–58
life support issues. *See* durable
    power of attorney for health
    care (DPAHC)
living wills, 78
long-term care, 2–3, 45, 79–82
    chances of needing, 81, 83
    costs of, 2–3, 79–81, 83–84
    defined, 83
    family support, 86–87
    federal government involvement, 84–86
    gifting to qualify for Medicaid, 62, 65–66
    LTC insurance, 66, 82, 87–88
        adult day care, 93, 100
        alternative plan for care, 92
        benefit period, 89
        checklist for buyers, 98–102
        companies, consideration of, 100, 103
        costs of, 87–88, 89, 90–99
        custodial care, 100
        daily benefit, 88–90, 99
        date of policy, 102
        elimination period, 90, 101

long-term care (*cont.*)
finding the right plan (checklist),
100–102
"free look" period, 101
group and individual plans, comparison of, 93–94
guaranteed renewable clause, 94–95,
101
home health care, 91, 92, 100
income considerations, 88, 99
indemnity basis, 101–2
inflation option, 89–90
medical history, 102
nonforfeiture benefit, 91
organizations to contact, 103
outline of coverage, 101
preexisting conditions, 101
premium payment, 93, 94, 95–96, 101
professional advice regarding, 102–3
qualifications for care, 92–93, 100–101
restoration of benefits feature, 102
spousal discount, 92
state partnership arrangements, 82
tax or other laws affecting, 102
when to buy, 95–98
Medicare/Medicaid coverage, 81, 83–86
skilled nursing care, 85, 87

M
Medicaid, 33, 81–82
eligibility for, 65
gifting to qualify for, 62, 65–66
and long-term care, 81, 84, 85–86
Medicare, 81, 83–85
Medigap policies, 83–84
monthly expenses, 12
debt reorganization. *See* debt reorganization
early retirement considerations, 118–20
surviving spouse, increase in expenses
for, 138–40
mortgages. *See also* home
paying off mortgages to reduce debt, 179,
191
reverse mortgages. *See* reverse mortgages

N
National Association of Securities
Dealers (NASD), 11, 18, 21

O
optical insurance 116–17
outright gifting. *See* gifting

P
pension plans
early retirement considerations. *See* early
retirement
joint and survivor benefits. *See* joint and
survivor benefits
retirement savings plans. *See* retirement
plans
tax withholding from payments,
187–88
probate, 26–30, 32, 33, 41
affidavit, 33
gifting to avoid, 62, 64

Q
qualified retirement plans. *See*
retirement plans

R
refinancing of home. *See* home
remarriage of parent, 49–50, 56–58
retirement plans
early retirement considerations. *See* early
retirement
employer pension plans. *See* pension
plans
401K plans, 106, 107–13
IRAs, 113, 125–26, 129–30,
132–33
tax on withdrawals, 107–8, 125–33
reverse mortgages, 181
advantages of, 181
FHA reverse mortgages, 182–83
gifting, effect of, 66
joint tenancy and, 54
organizations and information on,
183–84

qualifications, 181–82
types of, 182
risk, 10, 17

S
savings accounts
    retirement savings plans. *See* retirement
        plans
    in trust, 37
SEPP payments. *See* early retirement
Social Security
    for divorced surviving spouse, 191
    estimates of benefits, 12
    home paid off prior to, 191
    at sixty-two or sixty-five, 188–89
    for surviving spouse, 136, 139–40, 190–91
    working after, 189–90
surviving spouse
    home as asset for, 135, 139, 140
    increase in expenses for, 138–40
    joint and survivor benefits for. *See* joint
        and survivor benefits
    joint tenancy with right of survivorship.
        See joint tenancy WROS
    and life insurance alternatives. *See* life
        insurance
    retirement plan tax averaging, spousal
        privilege for, 129
    Social Security benefits for, 136, 139–40,
        190–91
    trust and will considerations. *See* trusts
        and wills
    women disadvantaged, 140–41
survivorship, right of. *See* joint
    tenancy WROS

T
taxes
    estate taxes. *See* estate taxes
    estimated payment method, 188
    gifting, disadvantages of, 64, 65, 66
    gift taxes, 52–53, 66–67
    income taxes. *See* income taxes
    joint tenancy WROS, consequences of,
        52–53

pension payments, withholding from,
    187–88
refinancing home, 173
on retirement accounts, 107–8, 125–33
for surviving spouse, 139
trusts and wills, 2, 22–25
    A-B or marital trusts, 25, 40–43, 46
    advice in writing, 35
    attorneys for trust preparation, 34–36,
        43–48, 193
    backup will, 47
    beneficiary defined, 31
    change and control of trust, 36–37
    charitable remainder trust, 192–93
    checking and savings accounts in trust's
        name, 37
    comparison of trust and will, 32–33
    conservatorships, 29, 53–54
    death of spouse, trust alterations after, 58
    definitions, 31–32
    disadvantages of wills alone, 26–30
    document storage, 39
    do-it-yourself, 34
    durable power of attorney for health
        care, 47, 77. *See also* durable power of
        attorney for health care (DPAHC)
    estate taxes, 22–25, 30, 39–43
    fees, 26–27
    funding the trust, 47
    gifting, advantages of trusts over,
        63–67
    guardianship issue, 29–30
    incapacity or incompetence, trust
        provision for, 47
    income taxes for probate estate, 30
    income taxes for trust, 39
    intestate, 58
    irrevocable trust, 36
    joint tenancy with right of survivorship.
        See joint tenancy WROS
    marital or A-B trusts, 25, 40–43, 46
    override by joint tenancy WROS, 49–51,
        56–58
    preparation of, 32–33
    probate, 26–30, 32, 33, 41

trusts and wills (*cont.*)
  purpose of revocable living trust, 36
  reasons for will, 33
  refinancing of home in trust, 37
  revocable living trust, 31, 36, 41, 45
  size of estate, 34
  successor trustee, 31, 36
  testamentary trust, 41

trustees, appointment of, 37–38
trustor and trustee defined, 31
updating trust, 39
who should have trust, 33–34

W
wills. *See* trusts and wills
wrap accounts, 16

ABOUT THE AUTHORS

After considerable experience with Wall Street financial institutions, **Suze Orman** created the Suze Orman Financial Group where she works with individuals and major corporations in retirement planning.

As a specialist in retirement issues and a Certified Financial Planner, Orman has appeared regularly on CNN, CNBC, QVC, and *Fox After Breakfast*.

For fourteen years Orman gave retirement planning seminars for one of Northern California's major employers. She has also served as expert witness in security fraud and insurance cases involving the negligent actions of major brokerage/insurance firms against the elderly.

She is the author of *You've Earned It, Don't Lose It* and *The 9 Steps To Financial Freedom*, and contributes a monthly column to *Self* Magazine. A University of Illinois graduate in social work and Chicago native, she now lives in Oakland, California.

Linda Mead is a writer and editor based in San Francisco.